SECURE FINANCIAL FUTURE INVESTING IN REAL ESTATE

MARTIN STONE
SPENCER STRAUSS

Dearborn™
Trade Publishing
A **Kaplan Professional** Company

Vice President and Publisher: Cynthia A. Zigmund
Senior Managing Editor: Jack Kiburz
Interior Design: Lucy Jenkins
Cover Design: Design Solutions
Typesetting: Elizabeth Pitts

© 2003 by Martin Stone and Spencer Strauss

Published by Dearborn Trade Publishing
A Kaplan Professional Company

Printed in the United States of America

03 04 05 06 07 10 9 8 7 6 5 4 3 2

Library of Congress Cataloging-in-Publication Data

Stone, Martin.
    Secure your financial future investing in real estate / Martin Stone
and Spencer Strauss.
        p.   cm.
Includes index.
    ISBN 0-7931-6129-0 (7.25 × 9 paperback)
1. Real estate investment.   I. Strauss, Spencer.   II. Title.
HD1382.5 .S76   2003
332.63'24—dc21

                                                                2002154703

Dearborn Trade books are available at special quantity discounts to use for sales promotions, employee premiums, or educational purposes. Please call our Special Sales Department to order or for more information, at 800-621-9621, ext. 4404, or e-mail trade@dearborn.com.

DEDICATION

MARTIN STONE: To Aaron, Chris, and Adam—in the hopes that they use my experiences and words to accomplish all their dreams.

SPENCER STRAUSS: For my brothers Larry and Steve—who have always been my best friends and biggest fans.

CONTENTS

PREFACE

There are more than 5,000 books listed on Amazon.com on the subject of real estate. By reading any of them, you can learn how to buy property, manage it, fix it, trade it, and sell it, as well as a host of countless other savvy maneuvers. Regrettably, what's missing in the lion's share of these books are chapters devoted to teaching the reader about the most compelling reasons to invest—that is, recognizing the long-term financial benefits to owning property and then, and most important, learning how to use those benefits to fund the kind of life and, ultimately, the kind of retirement everyone truly desires. Our plan is to tackle these aspects of the real estate game head-on.

The birth of this book came about from lessons we learned in two distinct areas. The first was in our everyday business as real estate brokers, selling investment property to people like you for more than 30 years. The second was in the reaction to our first published book, *The Unofficial Guide to Real Estate Investing* (Wylie, 2000). We were confident that if that book did its job, then everyone who read it would beg, borrow, or steal enough money for a down payment and run out and buy a small set of units. Why? Simple, because we know through experience that investing in real estate is a truly effective route to a secure financial future. You don't need a wheelbarrow full of money, a string of hot stock tips, or a Harvard MBA to succeed in this arena. Rather, you just need a willingness to learn and a modest amount of gumption to agree to put your feet in the water.

Unfortunately, our experience showed that it was mostly those who possessed a true entrepreneurial spirit before they bought our book who were the ones who took the risk and invested after they had read it. Their backgrounds and situations varied, but one common denominator stood out: The flame of ambition and desire to take control of their finances had been lit long before they had ever read our book. Our first book simply gave them the road map they'd been searching for.

Sure, we managed to reel in a number of additional converts along the way. In fact, we personally helped to create more than a few small empires over the years for some readers who were committed to someday retiring from the rat race. But by and large, even people who raved about our content, wrote glowing reviews on the Internet, and came to learn from us at book signings often confessed that they just hadn't made up their minds to invest yet. This was troubling.

Walk into any bookstore and you'll see shelves full of books (including ours) promising to make you wealthy using this system or that. In fact, lots of books offer sound advice on how to build wealth in many arenas, not just real estate. We concluded that the problem is most books on this subject are offering a road map to riches to people who aren't truly committed to the trip. To that end, our number one goal in this book is to help light your flame of desire, to spark a burning ambition in you to take control of your future. We truly believe, especially in this post–WorldCom, post–

Enron era, the stakes couldn't be higher. In fact, anything less may keep you working nine-to-five well beyond 65.

For many busy working people, saving money and thinking about setting up a retirement plan is the last thing they want to consider. They're pulling in a decent paycheck every week, spending it on bills and pleasure, and because they're young and energetic, they're confident that they can keep that train running for as long as necessary. Hopefully, something kicks in—let's call it maturity—and they realize what a dead-end merry-go-round they're on. Now, investing a portion of their salary toward a fruitful future becomes a top priority. Better late than never, right?

At this point, most working people willingly turn over the critical component of retirement planning to someone else—usually a stranger—whether it's the government through Social Security, their company's pension plan, a 401(k), or a similar arrangement administered by some expert. Regrettably, even a cursory look at any newspaper over the last year will show that most of these retirement vehicles administered by so-called experts come with serious problems. The Enron and WorldCom debacles speak volumes for the security (or lack thereof) of any company pension plan. As for Social Security, when our turn comes, at best it will provide us with a modest supplement to what is needed; at worst it will be nothing but a cruel joke.

What we're getting to is this: Unless you were born with the privilege of, for example, Prince William, you absolutely need to begin investing to protect you and your family in your retirement years. Statistics show that for almost 95 percent of all retirees, there's no golf club membership, no exciting vacations to those places you saw in the travel posters at the credit union, and no rest for the weary. You'd like to help your kids with college or to help them purchase their first home, but the truth is you'll be lucky to keep yours. Sadly, the blessing of abundance in our country has created a generation of people who believe everything is going to work out just fine in the end. The sad truth is, it's not.

Many people spend a good deal of time planning the profitability of the companies they work for, yet do nothing to create the same kind of security for their own families. Often, it's not until they get the ax because of company cutbacks that they realize it's too late. Or worse yet, they don't wake up until after they get a gold watch and a round of "For He's a Jolly Good Fellow." The reality is that once the novelty of being home during the day wears off, your spouse will get pretty tired of seeing you hanging around every day—because in retirement in the 2000s that's the only place you may be able to afford to go.

Everyone has read about the "golden parachutes" that executives get when they leave major companies. Those executives planned for those parachutes when they started their jobs. In fact, without a guarantee of one on the way out, they refused to take the job. Now check with the human resources department where you're working; did anyone create a golden parachute to help protect you when your tenure is over? The truth is there probably is the equivalent of a small umbrella set aside for you, if anything. Two weeks severance pay for years of service is hardly what we'd call "golden." As mentioned, you'll get an even smaller umbrella from Social Security—not very comforting after a lifetime of work. Our plan here is to show you how to create your own golden parachute via investments in real estate. It can be done. We've done it for ourselves, and we've helped countless others do it for themselves. Stick around.

Take this simple illustration: Many people would agree that the most successful investment they have ever made has been the purchase of their home. Over their years of ownership they've seen how their equity position in their house has magically flourished. They didn't need to do anything special; they only had to stay invested for the long haul. For these same people, however, the light has still never gone on. That is, they never seem to equate this profitable piece of real estate with the rest of their investment portfolio. What's more, they fail to recognize how a few additional smart real estate purchases over the next few years could set them up financially for a truly plentiful future. If you did so well owning your house for 10 or 20 years, think of the nest egg you could have accumulated by now had you just bought a few additional small units along the way.

This kind of thinking is the best way to prepare yourself for financial security and, ultimately, your eventual retirement. We're not talking about getting rich or making a killing flipping fixer-uppers or buying foreclosures. There are plenty of other books on the market to help you do those things. What's more, we'll tell you up front that this is not a get-rich-quick book. This is because real estate, by nature, is not a get-rich-quick investment. Our purpose here is to help you create something much more real and tangible than that—long-term security for you and your family. We've done it for ourselves, we've helped others do it, and with this book we're going to teach you how to do it.

The plan is to educate you in the same conservative investment techniques that we have espoused to our readers and clients for the past quarter of a century. Here, we'll teach you that success in real estate doesn't take smoke, doesn't include mirrors, and doesn't require luck. Rather, success here simply requires a well-thought-out road map. The good news is that the nucleus of your road map is now resting in your hands. These techniques have helped to provide a cushy retirement for many an investor.

Thomas Jefferson once said, "Most people believe that they'll wake up some day and find themselves rich." Actually, Jefferson got it half right—eventually people do wake up, yet, unfortunately, when they do it's usually too late. Our hope is that you grab the ideas in this book, couple them with your own dreams, and make something fantastic happen before time runs out.

ACKNOWLEDGMENTS

The authors would like to express our most sincere appreciation to the following people: Lori Stone, Sandi Strauss, Maria Strauss, Larry Strauss, Blake Mitchell, Robert Fagan, Seymour Fagan, Kirk Melton, Adam Feldman, Tony Picciolo, Kerry Daveline, Aaron Cook, Ben Walton, Hans Harder, Valerie Decker, Jeremy Laws, Shelly Stone, and our agent, Sheree Bykofsky. You all helped in so many special ways. Thank you.

The following real estate professionals also lent a hand and to them we are grateful: Kathy Schuler at Prestige Realty in Inglewood, Colorado; James H. Marr at Marr Real Estate in Winthrop, Massachusetts; Larry Lick at Rental Housing Online (rhol.org) in Port Huron, Michigan; Carmen Martinez at Cardinal Pacific Escrow in Long Beach, California; and Mel Samick at Excalibur Mortgage in Huntington Beach, California. Thanks to all of you.

We would also like to extend our appreciation to all the staff at Dearborn Trade Publishing, including Cynthia Zigmund, Paul Mallon, Robin Bermel, Leslie Banks, Kay Stanish, and Jack Kiburz. We would also thank Mary B. Good for her initial interest in our idea and then by introducing us to the great Don Hull. Speaking of Don Hull, we would like to thank him for championing this book and supporting us every step of the way. What a great guy.

Finally, a special thank you goes out to Steven D. Strauss, Glenn Bozarth, Chris Stone, and Jay Treat. We thank them for their edits, charts, rewrites, contributions, ideas, friendship, and never-ending support.

Back-cover photographs are courtesy of Jeff Eichen at Eichen Imagine Photography in Los Angeles.

CHAPTER 1

RETIREMENT REALITIES

"Lack of money is the root of all evil."
—GEORGE BERNARD SHAW

Most aspects of our modern culture focus primarily on immediate gratification. The idea of planning ahead for retirement, therefore, isn't very appealing. For that reason, most of us race through our lives acting as if a retirement fund will simply take care of itself. This laissez-faire attitude towards planning for the future was especially true when we were younger—probably because when we were new in the working world, we were too busy stretching our newfound wings of freedom. When we were young and invincible, nothing could harm us and nothing could stop us.

In those years the possibility of failure and of not being rich never even entered our minds. Sure, our parents and mentors tried to warn us about what lay ahead. But in truth, most of us went on living our lives thinking and acting as if we always knew best. Because we were so much smarter than our parents, we had little doubt that we would succeed.

Eventually, we came to understand that becoming a mature and responsible adult wasn't as easy as we thought. "Why," we ask, "didn't the folks hold our feet to the fire on some truly important things that would have made a real difference to us?" Where were the lessons about savings and investing for a safe future? Perhaps it was because our parents had their own troubles. They were probably so caught up trying to salvage their own dreams they didn't have anything left to help us with ours. Even more likely is that after leaving their own youth and dreams behind, they spent the remainder of their lives in survival mode. In reality, most parents probably just lacked the money to pay for the things that they would have liked to do or have (for themselves and for us). Empty bank accounts as senior citizens simply left them drained, both emotionally and financially.

TIME COSTS MONEY

In Lionel Bart's musical *Oliver!,* Fagin sings, "In this life, one thing counts, in the bank, large amounts." Truer words, especially for anyone who has hopes of hanging up his or her hat for good one day, have never been spoken. It's ironic, however, that most of the truly important things in life are usually free: watching a sunset with someone we love, having the time to help coach our child's soccer game, or being home when the kids get out of school to help with homework. MasterCard calls these things "priceless." On the other hand, do any of us have fond memories of the countless hours of overtime we put in over the years at work?

So what's the message? Salesmen say, "Time is money." In this instance, time costs money, for it takes money to pay for the time we need to achieve the things that are truly important. Second, and equally important, if we don't take the time early on to plan to make that money, nobody else will. The money isn't going to magically appear from the company pension plan, government and Social Security benefits won't make a dent, and winning the lottery is nothing more than a pipe dream. Instead, if we are to enjoy a fruitful life after we're finished working, we have to plan to make it ourselves.

THE STATS DON'T LIE

Years ago we received a copy of a report from the Continental Airlines Federal Credit Union. In it Continental implored its employees to begin saving for retirement. The headline from almost 30 years ago gave its employees some staggering food for thought. It read:

Retirement Facts

Of every 100 people retiring at age 65,

- Ninety-five percent are practically broke.
- Twenty-three percent must continue to work.
- Two percent are financially independent.
- Of these same 100 people, almost 75 depend on friends, family, or charity.

That was almost 30 years ago, back when it was certainly easier to make ends meet for the average worker. In those years, families could afford to survive on a single salary. While one parent worked, the other stayed home and cared for the children. The outlook today, however, is vastly different. Now it usually takes at least two incomes to keep a family afloat. As for children, because of the economics of today's world, many are being raised in childcare, which doesn't come cheap. These costs, coupled with everything else it takes to stay above the waterline, have kept most Americans living day to day and paycheck to paycheck.

Given these frightening statistics, here is some present-day food for thought: If 30 years ago stats showed that only 2 percent of those retiring were financially independent, what might the figures be today assuming things are getting worse? If 30 years ago a whopping 95 percent (95 percent!) of those retiring were practically broke, then what might the number be when it comes time for you to retire? The answers are self-evident. All this is in light of the fact that we live in the greatest country on earth when it comes to providing the opportunity to succeed. The beauty of America is that each of us can achieve just about anything we want—including a comfortable retirement—but we must exert the effort.

INFLATION: FRIEND OR FOE?

Though the past is no guarantee of the future, often it's a pretty solid indicator of the direction in which we might be headed. Here's an illustration of just how quickly inflation has changed the economics of retirement planning for the worse. In a November 1990 *Los Angeles Times* story entitled "The Key to Retirement Planning: Start Early," experts agreed that in retirement most Americans will need 70 to 80 percent of their preretirement income each year to maintain their current standard of living.

Ten years later, in July of 2000, *Business Week* magazine trumped those numbers with some of its own. It reported that planners now believe that 70 to 80 percent was just a bare-bones estimate. Now, it concluded, Americans interested in retiring someday should plan on generating 100 percent of what they spend currently.

As you can see, the ten years between 1990 and 2000 required a major overhaul in the thinking of how much money one needed to put aside to maintain a preretirement standard of living. And remember, this was the amount of money needed just to maintain a current standard of living. It bore no resemblance to the amount it would cost to fund any extra fun you might like to have in those years.

For most of us, we spend our days getting ready for the day, working, having dinner and watching television, and then doing it all over again. We do this for 50 or so weeks a year. We get a day off here or there, a few extra days for holidays and a week or two off for our annual vacation. The trouble is, in retirement we're going to have a lot more free time. And as we're learning, time costs money. But if our nest egg is only big enough to maintain our previous life-style, how will we fund anything extra we'd like to do? Like time, fun costs money, too. Even municipal golf isn't cheap, let alone air-fares, hotel rooms, and dinner out. We would all like to own a cabin or beach house or RV, but these things also cost.

The lesson here is that inflation will probably be our biggest enemy in preparing for retirement. What's more, if simple inflation weren't bad enough, the U.S. Bureau of Labor statistics now tell us that inflation can be even worse for seniors. This governmental bureau started tracking prices for Americans over 62 in an index called the CPI-E. Since December of 1982, this index has increased 3.5 percent on an annual average as compared to 3.3 percent for the regular consumer. Experts believe that these higher living expenses are almost entirely the result of increased health care costs.

The price of medical care is something that cannot be over-looked when planning for the future. The good news is that even though medical care costs more, the care itself is also significantly better. Consequently, we're all living longer and healthier lives.

For many young people the thought of living to be 80 or more is incomprehensible. But because of recent medical advances, most will. In fact, many financial planners today take the conservative approach and would like their clients to accumulate enough assets so they can live to be 95 years old without running out of money. Ninety-five! As it stands now, most of us can't survive until the next paycheck without running out of money, let alone to 95!

Close your eyes for a moment and just think what it might be like to live to a ripe old age. You thought you did everything right in life. You were responsible, raised children, worked hard for 40 years, saved and invested as much as you could in the stock market, and took good care of your health. You're now 80 or 90 years old. Sadly, because of poor planning, fear, inflation, and debacles like the Enron disaster, you are now among the 95 percent of the population that is practically broke. If you're lucky, your children or friends are caring for you. If you're not, you're on your own.

You may be thinking that it can't be all that bad. Well, let's see. Here's a simple exercise to help determine how close to reality these fact might be. Most of us probably work in a field where we can look up the names and phone numbers of a few people that retired, say 5, 10, or even 20 years ago, from a job similar to yours. If you work in a bigger company, the human resources department may be able to help find some people to talk to. The task is to call these people and ask them how their retirement is going. Specifically, ask how the company retirement plan is working. How much is Social Security helping them out? Is their retirement all it's cracked up to be? Do they wish they would have made some different choices regarding investing along the way? Odds are, your former colleagues will give you a quick dose of their own brand of retirement reality.

If you have the courage to follow through with this exercise, we think you will fully understand why it's time to get involved in running your own retirement program—a program independent of any Social Security benefits you're counting on or your company pension plan.

INFLATION AND THE FIXED INCOME

We've discussed inflation and its effects on your future. We will be showing you later how inflation can be your new best friend as a real estate investor. That is, if you learn how to harness its effects for your own good. For now we want to help you understand why inflation has such a devastating effect on most Americans, especially those who are retired and on a fixed income.

So, what is inflation? In simple terms inflation is the loss in purchasing power of the money you have. Countless textbooks have been written about the subject, but for the average American, inflation can be defined as how much stuff that money in your wallet will buy.

During our working years the effects of inflation are often minimized by cost-of-living adjustments and other compensations from an employer. What's more, as we grow in the workplace most of us strive to continually improve ourselves. As we receive raises in salary or get new jobs that provide better pay, it appears as though we begin to spend at a slower rate. Therefore, the effects of inflation aren't so noticeable. In these years, we settle into midlife, and we actually gain a false sense of security because our expenses seem to stabilize or, in some cases, even decrease. Once we retire, however, we won't have that inflation-hedging job anymore. It's at that point that we start using up our nest egg to support ourselves and this is where the truly harsh effects of inflation really begin to kick in.

Figure 1.1 is a chart of the historical inflation rates since 1975. These figures are unnerving, for when it comes time for you to retire, you might live long enough to see just as many swings in the rate.

For the majority of us, most of our retirement income will come from money in various investments that hopefully are still earning a profit. The challenge facing us is to be sure we have a large pot of money and can earn enough to pay our expenses and protect any nest egg we've accumulated from the effects of inflation.

Inflation affects the cost of just about everything. If we make enough on our investments to pay our bills, then our nest egg is secure. If inflation outpaces our earnings, then we have to use up some of the principal to live on. As we use up the principal, the

FIGURE 1.1
HISTORICAL INFLATION RATES, 1975–2002

Year	Inflation Rate
1975	6.94
1976	4.86
1977	6.70
1978	9.02
1979	13.29
1980	12.52
1981	8.92
1982	3.83
1983	3.79
1984	3.95
1985	3.80
1986	1.10
1987	4.43
1988	4.42
1989	4.65
1990	6.11
1991	3.06
1992	2.90
1993	2.75
1994	2.67
1995	2.54
1996	3.32
1997	1.70
1998	1.61
1999	2.68
2000	3.39
2001	2.86
2002	1.59

remaining balance declines and we need to take out even more to pay the bills. At some point the nest egg will be used up. This is the unfortunate situation of the 95 percent of retirees who are broke.

THE TAX MAN COMETH

There's another component to this equation: taxes. Because your nest egg will be invested, you will need to pay taxes when you take out most of the earnings. These laws can be very complicated so it would be worth your time to seek out an expert to answer your specific questions. Here, however, our goal is to show you the effect of inflation and taxes on what you really earn on those investments.

Just as inflation can fluctuate, so does the return you can expect on your investments. As we write this in early 2002, most banks are paying near 2 percent or lower on certificates of deposit (CDs). This doesn't even keep pace with inflation.

To illustrate, we'll use the following example: For inflation we'll use 3 percent, for your return on investments we'll use 7 percent, and for taxes we'll use 28 percent. What we're looking for is actual growth in the purchasing power of your nest egg or, at least, the ability to protect the principal balance. We'll assume you have $50,000 earning 7 percent.

The bottom-line numbers look like this:

Nest Egg	$50,000
Rate of Return	× 7%
Earnings	$ 3,500

Then multiply the earnings by the tax bracket to determine how much tax is owed:

Earnings	$ 3,500
Tax Rate	× 28%
Tax Owed	$ 980

To determine the loss in purchasing power because of inflation, multiply the nest egg by the inflation rate:

Nest Egg	$50,000
Inflation	× 3%
Loss in Purchasing Power	$ 1,500

In order to determine the actual rate of return, subtract your taxes owed and your loss in purchasing power from your earnings:

Earnings	$3,500
Less Taxes	− $ 980
Less Loss in Purchasing Power	− $1,500
Real Return	$1,020

Finally, to determine your percentage return on your investment, divide the return by the nest egg:

$$\$1,020 \text{ (Return)} \div \$50,000 \text{ (Nest Egg)} = 2.04\%$$

As you can see, a 2.04 percent return isn't a very comforting margin of error, especially when it comes to protecting the nest egg that will support you and your family for the rest of your lives.

We're sure you have watched inflation go up several times in your life and marveled at how slowly the yields on your investments caught up to the increases. It's at those times that retired Americans either dip into their nest eggs to live or are forced to seriously cut back on their current standards of living to preserve them.

SOCIAL SECURITY

A frequent topic of conversation when discussing retirement is Social Security. Most people joke about Social Security, nervously admitting that they doubt it will be around when their turn to retire comes. But for our parents and grandparents, Social Security has been one of those staples in life on which they've come to truly depend. Though not a huge amount, the monthly check in the mail has been the only thing that keeps many older Americans clothed and fed. In truth, most Americans believe that the government will come through when it's their turn. Sadly, the joke will probably be on all of us.

For Social Security to remain solvent and offer some meager help, major changes must be made in the system. Those changes will most likely include a combination of raising the withholding tax, increasing the age when benefits start, or limiting the benefits to those with other sources of retirement income—none of which hardly seems fair. Nonetheless, regardless of what the changes are, or when the changes take place, changes must happen for the system to survive.

Here are some facts about the program: Social Security began in 1935. At that time the standard retirement age was 65, yet the life expectancy of a man in those years was just 63. The government as you can see was pretty clever. This kind of math would have made the oddsmakers in Las Vegas swoon. When comparing the amount of money paid in versus the probable amount that needed to be paid out, Uncle Sam stood to make out like a bandit.

Social Security is the primary source of income for more than 60 percent of Americans 65 or older. For more than 25 percent of that same group, those benefits represent 90 percent of their retirement earnings. Today, in 2002, the maximum benefit for one worker is $1,536 per month. For a couple, the amount increases to $2,304 per month. If you put these meager numbers together with the increase in life expectancy and factor in inflation, the outlook that Social Security will provide Americans with any breathing room is just short of laughable.

401(K)s

Besides the cruel joke that Social Security has become, the dream of a fruitful 401(k) to lead you to the promised land has also crashed and burned. Here's the scoop: In 1974 the Employee Retirement Income Security Act (ERISA) was enacted to reform traditional pension plans. Through this act, 401(k)s were created. To ensure that retirement plans were safe and diversified, ERISA mandated that no more than 10 percent of a plan's assets could be invested in company stock. As you might have guessed, someone discovered a loophole in this 10 percent mandate. Sadly, this lack of diversification spelled doom for many Americans in the early 2000s.

Many workers nearing retirement have watched helplessly as their nest eggs have suffered tremendous losses. Because they were overinvested, they could only sit helplessly on the sidelines and watch as their companies filed for bankruptcy and ceased to exist. Others listened to the tales of great gains at cocktail parties and invested heavily in temporarily lucrative areas associated with high tech or the Internet. As the dot-com bubble burst, their nest eggs cracked or broke all together.

The 401(k)s can give you a fantastic head start toward retirement, especially when it comes to taking advantage of the tax advantages these vehicles offer. However, any expert will attest that a balanced portfolio is a key component to successful planning, and this includes investing in a 401(k) plan if possible. The trouble comes from putting all your trust and money with anyone besides yourself. Clearly the spirit and heart of ERISA were lost once it became commonplace to invest more than 10 percent in these plans. But it wasn't just the loopholes that caused the problems; it was the fact that the owners of these dollars gave up control of their money to complete strangers. No wonder things went awry.

The secret to success with a 401(k), real estate, and any investment comes from possessing knowledge and control. It's your money and you're responsible for it. Certainly you need guidance from experts, but when it comes to your money you must remember that you are the CFO of your funds. You need to educate yourself and play a part in deciding where your money is being invested. Philip Oxley, the president of Tenneco, once said, "People who are going to be good managers need to have a practical understanding of the crafts in their business."

HEALTH INSURANCE AND RELATED NEEDS

Probably the most crucial consideration in planning for your retirement years will be addressing future medical needs. Regardless of how healthy we may be today, the day will come when the most critical issues in our lives will be about our health or that of a loved one. When we're healthy, about the only thing we think about is which insurance program will be the least expensive. When we get sick, however, this now becomes, I want the best open-heart specialist working on me. Unfortunately, at that point it's too late. We'll get what our insurance company agrees to pay for and that's that.

Because the costs of providing health insurance are increasing at an alarming rate, more and more companies are finding new ways to limit their costs. Medical care provided by HMOs, PPOs, and large medical groups now seems to be the rule rather than the exception. In addition, more employers are passing on a good portion of the health insurance premiums to the employee. This isn't a problem as long as we're still working. But what happens if we lose our job or retire before other benefits like Medicare kick in?

Regardless of your present age, it would be a good exercise at this point to call your insurance agent and price a health policy for you and your family. Make sure you also get a price quote for the cost of insurance if you were 55 and another if you were 65. At this point you will start to get an idea of what the cost would be if you lost your insurance from your job, or you retired early and had to pick up the tab yourself.

Once we reach 65 we can look to Medicare to help supplement some of our health care needs. Medicare's coverage is limited, however, leaving us exposed in many ways. There are deductibles, copayments, and many health care expenses that aren't covered. Currently, Medicare doesn't pay for custodial care, out-of-pocket prescription drugs, or home health care. Worse yet, many doctors won't accept Medicare as payment in full. When this happens you have one of three choices. First, you can pay the difference directly to your doctor; second, you could change doctors; or finally, you could choose not to get treated at all. Fortunately, there are policies that you can buy to pay the part of the bill that Medicare doesn't cover. But again, that's an additional expense that will tap your nest egg month after month. As you can see, these extra benefits will be one of those long-term increasing expenses that will be critical to plan for.

The last health-related issue we need to mention is long-term care. This is perhaps the least understood coverage available today. Long-term health care is insurance that will provide care for a prolonged illness or disability. This usually encompasses services in a nursing facility or at home. Statistics now show that anyone who lives beyond 65 will have a high probability of spending some time in a nursing facility during his or her lifetime. Unfortunately, Medicare and the policies that complement Medicare are unlikely to cover the expenses associated with this kind of care. To pay for it, the money will probably have to come out-of-pocket.

The price of an extended stay in a nursing facility is staggering. In today's dollars, a year's stay in a nursing home can cost between $45,000 and $90,000, depending on the facility and the area of the country in which you reside. At these rates it's pretty easy to see why even paying for short stays can quickly deplete one's retirement fund. Alternatively, some coverage allows you to receive this kind of care within the comfort of your own home. But this doesn't come cheap. Nonetheless, at-home nursing care is now one of the most sought-after benefits of insurance coverage.

The thought of buying insurance for events that won't happen for another 20 or 30 years doesn't occur to most people. Nonetheless, as medical science makes further advances and life expectancy rates increase, the probability exists that we all may someday face soaring health costs.

As with other types of insurance, the premium changes drastically as you age. A couple in their middle 50s might pay 60 percent less per year than a couple in their middle 60s. Currently, experts in the field suggest that if your net worth is less than $200,000, you won't be able to afford this kind of insurance and will be left to fend for yourself.

LIFE EXPECTANCY

We've hinted at our increasing life expectancies earlier in this chapter. We feel that it's important to give you some concrete facts, for this is the primary reason that retirement planning is so important.

As we move from childhood to adulthood, our goals and desires in life change drastically. We are taught to find something we like to do and learn more about it in school so we can pick a career we enjoy. For many, this works out fine. We have talked to enough different people throughout our careers that we don't believe the majority of Americans are that happy going to work every day. Sure, a lucky few fell into careers they absolutely love. But for most, a job is just a job, a means to a paycheck and a better life.

FIGURE 1.2
LIFE EXPECTANCY CHART

Current Age	Expectant Age for Women	Expectant Age for Men
25 years old	81.3	76
35 years old	81.7	76.7
45 years old	82.2	77.7
55 years old	83.2	79.1
65 years old	84.9	81.6
75 years old	87.7	85.4
85 years old	92.1	90.8

Source: U.S. Department of Health and Human Services.

There's an old saying, "The worst day fishing is better than the best day working." Substitute your idea of a good time for fishing and you will understand what we mean. Our position is to do a better job of being the CEO of your family's finances, and you can pick the day you retire, and retire in style.

Figure 1.2 will give you an idea of how the numbers are stacking up today. Remember, if you are 30 years old, these numbers may change a lot in the next 30 years. If you were retiring today at 55, you have a good shot at being able to enjoy retirement for another 28 years. If you started working after college, your retirement years will number almost as many as your working years.

As you study the chart, think of how those years might be spent if you plan wisely today—golf, trips, second homes at the beach, or just being able to have the time and money to be with your friends, family, and kids. Now turn the tables on yourself and ponder what those years would be like living with empty pockets and limited resources. Unfortunately, that struggle is almost a guaranteed outcome for 95 percent of all Americans. But as we've noted, you can do something about it and we intend to show you how.

CHAPTER 2

GREAT EXPECTATIONS

*"The highest use of capital is not to make money,
but to make money do more for the betterment of life."*
—HENRY FORD

In his respected book, *Invest in Yourself: Six Secrets to a Rich Life,* Marc Eisenson notes that once we become adults, "We often lose track of life's simple pleasures and of our own personal goals. We take a wrong turn or two, then spend a good portion of our lives doing things we'd rather not—while not doing the things we'd enjoy." He goes on, "While we may obsess about how unhappy we are, we don't focus clearly on what we can do to change the situation, on how we can invest our time, energy, and, yes, our money to consciously create the life we want."

In this chapter we want to accomplish three things: First, we want to help get a handle on where we stand financially at this very moment. Second, we'll see what it will take to at least maintain our current lifestyle—how to generate that 80 to 100 percent of our current income needed once we're through working. Finally, we'll do some realistic dreaming about the kind of life we'd truly like to have. Like Eisenson said, there are ways we can invest our time, energy, and money to consciously create the life we want. Here, in Chapter 2, we'll consciously start down that road.

FOCUS UP

As you know, this is a book about using real estate as a retirement vehicle. We'll get to that. But as we said earlier, right now our goal is to get the attention of those who don't already "get" it and help focus on making those retirement years truly enjoyable. Any investment we choose is just a tool to help generate the money necessary to find or pay for happiness. Investing in real estate is no different, for it will be just a means to an end. It's like trading our time for dollars at our jobs. We don't get up every morning at 6:30 to be at work by 8 because we simply love entering data into a computer. Rather, we go to earn the money we need to generate the type of lifestyle we desire. It's an added bonus if we enjoy our jobs, but in the end it's all about the money.

As we get older, we learn that though our jobs may be about the money, our lives are certainly not. We mentioned earlier how it's those priceless things that usually hold the most meaning: coaching our son in his first Little League game or watching our daughter in a ballet recital wearing the dress we had the time to make. No, it's not just about the money. But, alas, money is the tool we need to obtain the things we really want. We didn't make up these rules, but they are the rules nonetheless.

At this point you're probably saying to yourself, If it's not about the money then why am I reading this book? What we're talking about is finding a balance in life. We want to strike a chord in your life so you will start actively thinking about creating something special for yourself in the future, as opposed to just living for the present.

FINDING BALANCE

When most of us make comments about the rich, we usually say things like: "Ah, they never have to work" or "They can do anything they want." Thus, we resent the wealthy without realizing that with a bit of planning our lives could be abundant as well. Success is about finding a balance between wanting what you don't have and being happy and content with what you do have. Poor people aren't always unhappy and rich people aren't always happy.

American author Whit Hobbs says that "Success is waking up in the morning, whoever you are, however old or young, and bouncing out of bed because there's something out there that you love to do. Something that you believe in, that you're good at—something that's bigger than you are, and you can hardly wait to get at it again." Hobbs doesn't talk about money or a job. He's talking about doing something every day that you love to do. Thus, money can't bring happiness. But it will provide the opportunity and wherewithal to find what you love to do.

It's the task of finding out where we would truly like to be that evades most of us. We get so caught up in surviving each day that we fail to make the time to remember what it is that really makes us happy. Worse yet, the things that probably would make us happy are with us daily, but we are so busy working at life that we fail to enjoy the happiness we do have. Remember the scene in the *Wizard of Oz* where everyone got their wish but Dorothy? The Tin Man was shown what a big heart he had, the Scarecrow realized that he was indeed the brains of the operation all along, and even the Cowardly Lion came to own his own bravery. For Dorothy, though, all hope seemed lost. That is until Glinda the Good Witch arrived. Glinda reminded Dorothy that she was wearing the slippers that would take her home all the time. Well, that's what we're talking about.

Isn't it possible that we're each wearing our own pair of ruby red slippers right now? To avoid chasing the wrong dreams, it's important to spend some time now determining what it is that will give you happiness and contentment in the future. Like Dorothy, a bit of focused thought on what it is we want might just send us home again. This is a book about making the money to pay the toll of life. This toll will help us secure the freedom to enjoy what makes us truly happy.

THREE STEPS

We will be presenting a couple of basic systems that should help in reaching your goals. Of course, these systems don't carry any guarantee, but by educating yourself you maximize your probability of success. The Boy Scouts got it right when they made their motto "Be prepared." This is advice that we all should take seriously for anything we do, but especially when dealing with our future.

Besides being prepared, the following three steps must be adhered to when it comes to investing. Each step is essential, and each one builds on the other:

1. Grow your investments.

2. Protect your investments.

3. Enjoy the fruits of your investing.

Growing your investments is the first goal. The rub is that by growing our investments we must put off that all-too-common human trait to consume. As Americans, statistics show that the majority of us spend roughly 110 percent of what we bring in each month. No wonder we can't get ahead. Now is the time to rethink that behavior. The idea is to deny ourselves a few present-day pleasures to achieve some loftier and more important goals for the future.

Protecting your investments is the second task. Because any profit is the return we earn for taking some level of risk, one can never have a foolproof investment. Nonetheless, if we do our homework properly and stay vigilant, we will realize the highest probability of success in reaching our goals. Thankfully, this probability of success is especially true when it comes to investing in real estate.

Finally, enjoying the fruits of your investments is what it's all about. In life, nothing is worth it unless there is a payoff at the finish line. With investments we call that payoff a profit. This is a critical component to this equation, but one that is all too often bypassed by the workaholic. For him or her, and for many of the rest of us, we need to remember why we are trying to make those profits. It's all too easy to get caught up in the growing phase of our investments and never take time out to enjoy the fruits of our labor. This attitude is just as risky as the attitude of those who only live for today.

The failure to stop and smell the roses is a very real problem. Our world is moving at an increasingly faster pace. It's at this clip that we forget who we are and what makes us happy. In a novel entitled *Divided Roads,* author Ned Mansour's main character, Pete, notes that "I have totally lost all sense of reality. The speed of the treadmill has constantly increased and the elevation has so heightened that I simply can't remember what it feels like to walk slowly on level ground and see the sights. I don't know if I have the determination it takes to recover." For Pete, and for many other Americans just like him, this feeling of being a caged hamster is all too prevalent.

To help free you from your cage, we hope that this book will motivate you to make some positive changes. But don't lose sight of what you're really after. It's all too easy to get paralyzed by where you are or the life you feel trapped in. This is especially true of people who have many responsibilities. We're not saying that being responsible is a bad trait, only that it tends to make us better at doing what others say we should do or be, rather than listening to what our heart tells us. The people that set the directions for the company that you work for know exactly what they want. Read on and discover their secrets.

DETERMINING NET WORTH

Before you can figure out where you're going, you should get a handle on where you sit financially today. The next few forms are pretty simple to fill out. The best way to find out where you are at this moment is to work up a balance sheet, which lists your assets and liabilities. Once you've completed your list, if you subtract your liabilities from your assets, the remainder will be your net worth. Your net worth is the sum total of what you have been able to save from all the money you have earned to date. Theoretically, these are the assets you will be able to put to work to earn you money when you retire. This money plus Social Security and any existing company retirement plan you may have will be the beginning of your nest egg. Don't fret if you discover that your nest egg is nil or next to nil at this point. The idea is just to get a handle on where you are at this moment.

Because the goal of this book is to get you to take advantage of the benefits of real estate, we suggest you complete a standard Federal National Mortgage Association (FNMA) 1003 loan application. You can get an FNMA (i.e., Fannie Mae) loan application at almost any bank, mortgage broker, or savings and loan that makes home loans. These forms are the standard in the industry and once put together with all the required schedules, they will save you a lot of time once you begin applying for real estate loans. Once completed, it will be easy to update any items that change over the years.

In lieu of a standard Fannie Mae loan application, you can start with the form in Figure 2.1 to help you determine your net worth.

FIGURE 2.1
NET WORTH SUMMARY

Home Equity (value less loans)	$_____
Vehicle Equity (value less loans; don't forget boats and toys)	$_____
Cash or Equivalents (savings, checking, money markets, etc.)	$_____
Stocks, Bonds, Mutual Funds	$_____
IRAs, Keoghs, 401(k)s	$_____
Equity in Life Insurance	$_____
Equity in Other Real Estate (value less loans)	$_____
Equity in Your Business	$_____
Art, Collections, Etc.	$_____
Other Assets	$_____
Total Net Worth	$_____

ASSETS VERSUS LIABILITIES

At this point it's important to begin to think about an important concept concerning assets and liabilities. The word *asset* implies something of value, as opposed to a liability, which refers to a debt. Regrettably, assets for retirement purposes are of value to you only if they provide a positive cash flow benefit. For instance, if you have a painting worth $5,000 hanging on your wall, it may give you pleasure, but pleasure aside, it's of no value to your retirement fund. That is, of course, unless you're charging admission to your neighbors for viewings. This is a primary concept you must understand: Unless the money you invest makes money, it becomes a liability.

The biggest negative value most of us have is our home. Sadly, like the Monet on your wall, the net equity from your home is of no value for retirement because it doesn't produce any spendable return. Furthermore, making the payment for taxes, insurance, upkeep, and a possible mortgage becomes a drain on the other incomes you have. Again, this negative drain makes your home not an asset but a liability.

The concept of considering a home a liability on a balance sheet rather than an asset is the most controversial and hotly debated subject we encounter in our business. But remember, our goal is to help you create enough income from real estate so you can afford all the dreams you care to pursue. To that end, this may require you to use the asset value of your home to jump-start your investment program.

If this thought gives you initial pause, just recall the statistics we quoted in the previous chapter. Ninety-five percent of all Americans retire practically broke—95 percent! If anything should scare you, that should. And because a good percentage of Americans own their own home, this statistic tells us that our home ownership could be in serious jeopardy if we don't do something to protect it before it's too late. Our goal isn't to talk you out of your home; rather, we want you to earn enough so you can always live wherever you want.

SPENDING HABITS

Now we want to take a look at your current spending habits. One of the secrets of growing your net worth is finding some extra money each month to help fund another investment (and another, and another, and another). The good news is that you can create this money by investing, working harder and/or smarter, or you can create it by saving. Either way, you'll have more on the bottom line.

Some people are lucky enough to already have a nest egg, but having money in the bank isn't necessary as long as you can learn to stay within a budget starting now. Again, we're not going to get into an extended budgeting lecture here. Our goal is to help you get a general idea of where you stand now and to realize that the earnings from your job should be used in two ways:

1. The money should be used to live and enjoy life.

2. Some money should be put aside so you can invest for a safe financial future.

We've adhered to the following investing advice throughout our careers and couldn't recommend it more highly. An anonymous author wrote, "Investing is simple: Get started, keep doing it, and never touch the principal."

The form in Figure 2.2 is designed to help you focus on all your regular monthly expenses. For most of us these expenses really control our financial lives. The secret to having more money on the bottom line for investments is getting control of, or eliminating, as many of your recurring monthly expenses as you can. For example, if you could manage to get your car paid off and forgo buying another brand-new one, you could have upwards of an extra $300 a month to put into an investment. Save that money for a year and you'll have accumulated $3,600 plus the interest you've earned in a money market account. Now you can use that to buy a $120,000 property with an FHA loan that requires only 3 percent down. The story just gets better and better, but that's what the rest of this book is about. So back to the budget.

Feel free to modify this format to suit your own expenses and lifestyle. The line items we listed are merely meant to start you thinking about how you spend the money you earn. Besides maintaining a budget manually, you can employ one of many computer programs to keep track of spending. These programs are effective and fun to play with, but, more important, work on finding ways

FIGURE 2.2
MONTHLY BUDGET

Income

Take-Home Pay	$_____
Other Income	$_____
Total	$_____

Monthly Expenses

Mortgage or Rent	$_____
Property Taxes	$_____
Income Taxes (not withheld)	$_____
Alimony, Child Support	$_____
Installment Debt	$_____
Credit Card Payments	$_____
Auto Insurance	$_____
Homeowners, Renters Insurance	$_____
Life Insurance	$_____
Health Insurance	$_____
Any Other Insurance	$_____
Savings	$_____
Food	$_____
Utilities	$_____
Home Maintenance	$_____
Auto Expenses	$_____
Daycare	$_____
Clothing/Cleaning	$_____
Personal Expenses, Hair/Gym	$_____
Medical/Dental Copay	$_____
Education	$_____
Entertainment/Vacations	$_____
Contributions	$_____
Spending Money	$_____
Miscellaneous	$_____
Total	$_____
Money Left Over for Investing	$_____

to save money for your investments. Remember, investments now will fund your fun later.

Pay particular attention to those expenses that you must pay every month—like car or boat payments, credit-card payments, and any other expenses that last for more than a year. Finding ways to lower or eliminate these expenses is the best way to find that extra money you need to start investing. Sure, when we fall in love with that new car or jetski, it's easy to go on the hook for the payments over three to five years. This is because new toys give us instant gratification. But remember, that new car wears out fast, but a solid investment will pay dividends for the rest of your life.

BACK TO THE FUTURE

Next we want to help you determine where you will be when it comes time for you to retire. We will make this review very simple. Again, our goal is to get you thinking about this subject—enough to give you an elementary education on what lies ahead.

The two main problems with predicting where you will be when you retire are:

1. Inflation

2. Job stability

Over time, inflation rates can change like the wind. In fact, at certain times inflation can actually be a friend, not a foe. You will learn later that if you have a lot of levered real estate in an inflationary time, your estate will grow at an astronomical rate. But if you've converted all your assets to cash and are trying to live off that in a low inflationary time, you're probably experiencing some financial problems. For this reason, we're going to try to determine where you will be in the future measured in today's dollars by factoring in 3 percent to account for inflation.

Estimating what you can expect from your pension plan can be a tough proposition. Because many companies seem to be disappearing at an alarming rate, it makes us wonder if those plans have any more value than depending on Social Security. One of our main themes thus far has been to help you recognize the shortcomings of relying on Social Security and your company pension plan. To help with that goal, we recommend you seek out what someone in your position would receive monetarily right now if he or she retired today with the number of years you will have on that job when you retire. You may need to make a few adjustments, but the idea is to get just a ballpark figure on the monthly amount.

Our goal from this exercise is specific. It's to make an estimate of any shortfall in retirement income if you don't do anything different from what you are already doing. We will then convert that shortfall to a lump-sum dollar figure (see Figure 2.3). This will give you a concrete goal to shoot for in your planning. To make this real easy, we suggest that you make it your goal to replace 100 percent of your current income.

To estimate that lump sum, we are going to assume that you will net only 3 percent on it. At the writing of this book, CD rates have been below 2 percent. With taxes and inflation, this certainly hasn't been a good time for cash investments. Surely this will improve, but if you're trying to sustain a 20- to 30-year retirement fund, we feel being conservative is best.

The table in Figure 2.4 is an estimate of the Social Security benefits you would receive in the future at full retirement age expressed in today's dollars. You can obtain more accurate information on your potential Social Security benefits by contacting Social Security directly at 1-800-772-1213 or at its Web site, <www.ssa.gov>.

FIGURE 2.3
RETIREMENT INCOME WORKSHEET

1. Annual Income Goal $_____
   (100% of your current income)

2. Estimated Social Security Benefits $_____

3. Estimated Pension Benefits $_____

4. Retirement Income Gap $_____
   (subtract lines 2 and 3 from line 1)

5. Lump Sum Needed $_____
   (divide amount on line 4 by .03)

6. Current Retirement Assets $_____
   (IRA, 401(k), and other sources)

7. Total Lump-Sum Gap $_____
   (subtract line 6 from line 5)

To use the table, find your earnings level on the left, and the chart will give you an idea on the right of your expected benefits.

As we mentioned earlier, this exercise is overly simplified to provide a basic understanding of what kind of retirement nest egg you are going to need. By relating the monthly income needed to a lump sum, we hope to help you visualize the task that lies ahead.

Many of you will have various types of assets that will provide you with a retirement income. Assets are great, but when you are retired and not bringing in a paycheck, all that really counts is the monthly income those assets may or may not generate. As mentioned earlier, if you have a lot of equity in your home and a valuable art collection you would rather not sell, neither can be used in calculating your lump-sum gap. In reality, these kinds of assets usually just increase the gap.

FIGURE 2.4
MONTHLY SOCIAL SECURITY BENEFITS IN TODAY'S DOLLARS

2005 Earnings	Benefits
$30,000	$ 906
$40,000	$1,094
$50,000	$1,281
$60,000	$1,469
Maximum	$1,822

DREAM A LITTLE DREAM

The following exercise is one that we hope will get you to act, and invest, differently. In all likelihood, if you've been working for 20 years and have accumulated a large deficit on the lump-sum line of the Retirement Income Worksheet in Figure 2.3, you're probably not going to accumulate the balance you need to retire the way you're going. So if you continue to do what you have done, you will be one of the 95 percent who are broke at retirement. Yes, you can sell the home or the paintings, but we don't believe you need to do that if you begin to invest properly for your retirement.

In reality, not only do we not want you to sell your home, we want you to start thinking about all the additional things you would like to have or do if you were retired and had the time and money. We're not just talking about dreaming here, we're talking about dreaming big. For many of you that lump-sum gap may seem so large that you're thinking it would be completely foolish to dream about other things at this point. Nothing could be further from the truth. Dreams are what make us truly live. We don't work hard because work is fun; we work hard to get the money to pay for the things that make us happy. The Reverend Robert Schuller said, "It's unfulfilled dreams that keep us alive."

FIGURE 2.5
SAMPLE WISH LIST

Dreams	Cost
Cabin	$100,000
Pleasure Boat	$ 25,000
New Car	$ 45,000
Country Club Membership	$ 25,000
Weekly Golf: $125/round for 10 Years	$ 62,500
Vacations: 4/year @ $2,500 Each	$100,000
College for Grandchildren: 3 @ $25,000	$ 75,000
Total Cost of Dreams	$432,500

Don't be discouraged if that lump-sum gap seems so huge that you'd feel foolish even thinking about "the better things in life." We have found that it's easier for most of us to sacrifice for something we "want to have" as opposed to something we "should be doing." We should all save money every month but do we? If you fall in love with that new car, just think how easy it was to justify that extra $200 a month to pay for it. In 20 years that car will be paid off and worth just a few thousand dollars. Rather than buy the car, if you had committed to putting the $200 in a bank account each month for those 20 years, you would have accumulated $48,000 by now.

Sit down with a paper and pen and start listing all the things you would like to enjoy when you retire. Don't forget anything. Henry David Thoreau said, "In the long run, we only hit what we aim at. Aim high." Aim high, so if you miss a few things along the way you'll still be a big winner. Figure 2.5 is a sample wish list and an estimate of what these kinds of dreams may cost.

Think we're crazy? You already have a lump-sum gap and now we're talking about adding almost half a million dollars to that figure! In Chapter 6, we will teach you in detail about the power of compound interest and leverage, and how real estate investing takes advantage of those simple principles. Here's a taste of how it works now. Let's say you have just 20 years to go before you retire and you determine you're short $100,000 on the lump sum. What's more, you now need to find another $432,500 to fund your wish list. Well, if you could get your hands on $30,000 to invest in real estate today and keep it growing at 20 percent per year for the next 20 years, your nest egg would grow to $1,150,128. We'd then discount that money at 3 percent to cover for inflation, and you still would have accumulated $636,798 in today's dollars. This amount of money definitely covers your lump-sum shortfall and still leaves you with a $100,000 cushion.

Is this guaranteed? Of course not, but would you rather take a chance on funding a comfortable retirement now and fulfilling your dreams or just waiting to wind up in the 95 percent broke group once you retire? This book is dedicated to giving you the best shot at fulfilling your dreams using real estate as the vehicle to get there.

CHAPTER 3

RETIREMENT STRATEGIES

"October: This is one of the particularly dangerous months to invest in stocks. Other dangerous months are July, January, September, April, November, May, March, June, December, August, and February."
—MARK TWAIN

We've spent the first two chapters imploring you to take charge of your financial future. As you've learned, the outlook for most is grim. There is an old saying about it never being too late, but the truth is, if you don't start planning for your future, it can be too late. If you believe the statistics, 95 percent of those eager to retire one day are on the road to nowhere.

STRIKING IT RICH

You've probably noticed that we've yet to talk about getting rich in this book. This is because getting rich is really a state of mind based on your definition of the word. "Rich" implies reaching a goal of obtaining a certain amount of money rather than actually achieving true desires and needs for you and your family. What's more, for an adult who is truly grounded, striking gold without hitting the lottery is simply beyond the realm of what is possible.

Now contrast "getting rich" with "practically broke." "Practically broke" is something many of us can remember, probably because we've all been there at one time or another. Truth be told, once we are no longer "practically broke," we never want to go back. We get a good job, start making decent money, and life is good. Even so, regardless of the variation on this theme, most of us believe that if we work hard enough our American dream will materialize. To that end we concluded Chapter 2 with a wish list for your retirement years. We tried to open your eyes to a retirement that could include second homes, golf vacations, water toys, and money to spare to help your grandchildren with their education. These types of perks may seem like pipe dreams, but they are absolutely attainable if you invest in real estate. Just ask anyone who's taken a chance and dipped their toes in this pool of water.

THREE GROUPS OF INVESTORS

To help distinguish the actions needed to achieve your dreams, we'll begin by categorizing you into one of three different groups. These groups are differentiated by the amount of years you have left to work and, conversely, by the number of years you'll be able to let your investments grow before you retire. Of course, everyone's story is different, but by picking three broad stages, we hope that everyone might find enough similarities in one of the groups to find a place to begin. These groups are:

1. "Got plenty of time": These people are in their 20s or early 30s and are just getting started working. For them, the world is their oyster. They believe that they can accomplish anything they set their minds to. Best of all, they have the benefit of time to help make their dreams come true.

2. "Too busy just hangin' on": These are baby boomers who are in the middle of their working lives. They have families, mortgages, and worries. Their prayer is that Social Security, a boom in the stock market, the company pension plan, or their children will help fill the bill when their retirement time comes. Their big fear is that they won't.

3. "Worried it may be too late": This is the over-50 crowd, and when it comes to retirement, they're scared to death. Statistics show that once they retire they'll probably have to go back to work as a greeter at their local Wal-Mart to make ends meet. Time is running out and they know it.

Thankfully, there is hope and, better yet, solutions for each of these groups, including group three. As authors and real estate investors, we have had plenty of personal experience living and succeeding through the stages of groups one and two. And professionally, as real estate brokers, we have helped countless people in the "it's probably too late" group fund comfortable retirements through real estate investing. We'll begin by talking to those who've "got plenty of time."

GROUP #1: "GOT PLENTY OF TIME"

We really don't get any smarter as we grow older; rather, we just gain experience from messing up so many times and not listening when we were younger. But the lessons we've learned haven't been all too different from those we learned in school. For example, in math class we learned that $2 + 2 = 4$. In the school of life we learn about math, too—specifically that too many credit-card payments can get you in a world of hurt. This is especially true when you're out of work or at any type of crossroads. A key difference between schoolhouse lessons and life lessons is that when you learn lessons in the real world, you tend to pay a bit closer attention. One reason is because real-world lessons often hit you where it hurts most: in the pocketbook.

In the movie *The Natural,* Glenn Close said, "We all have the life we learn with and the life we live with after that." We say you can decide to take your full measure of life and learn everything the hard way, or pay attention to what those who came before you have to pass on. Thankfully, there is good news: If you fit into this group you can accomplish almost anything that you put your mind to. This is primarily true because you have the time that will escape you once you get older: time to make mistakes, time to fix them, time to invest, and best of all, time to let your investments grow. If you use this time wisely, you will surely be able to live your dreams, not just dream about them, which is what so many other people have done.

Many just starting out feel like they have been misled by older people who didn't take advantage of the opportunities America has to offer. In truth, maybe some of the grown-ups in their lives were just a bit scared and therefore played it too safe along the way. Someone once said that you know you're old when your dreams turn to regrets. Napoleon Hill, the acclaimed author of *Think and Grow Rich,* couldn't disagree more. He said, "Cherish your visions and your dreams as they are the children of your soul, the blueprints of your ultimate achievements."

For those who've "got plenty of time," your financial future is like a rocket on a launchpad. However, it's up to you to decide which type of rocket you want to look like. Think about the rocket that launches the space shuttle into space. It leaves the launchpad slowly, builds up speed, and then boosts the space shuttle into orbit. As the photographs taken from the shuttle show, the view from up there is breathtaking. In contrast, a bottle rocket takes off very fast, rises a short distance, and then fizzles out and drops to earth. Ninety-five percent of those who retire in our country are like bottle rockets, yet only 5 percent are taking in that great view. True, they're not orbiting the earth from the space shuttle, but the view from the clubhouse at Pebble Beach is just as breathtaking.

As you begin making money it's tempting to spend not only the money you earn today but also to borrow on what you will make in the future: lots of dinners out on your charge card, a new car every few years, a big-screen TV financed at the credit union, and a tax refund loan to pay for a summer getaway. Yes, you can afford it. The problem is you get used to spending most (or all) of what you earn and not putting any away for your future. If this is you, you're headed for trouble.

To succeed and take advantage of real estate investing to help you reach your dreams, we're going to assume you'll agree to make a few small sacrifices early on. From there, we'll show you where those small sacrifices might take you from an investment standpoint. And because we don't want you to think you will have to sacrifice on this program forever, we are going to be working with just some of your earnings for the next five years. We'll make the following assumptions: You can save enough each year from your earnings and tax refund to invest $5,000 a year for those first five years. Additionally, instead of buying that new $25,000 car on credit, you will put the same amount as the payment into a savings account each month to be invested in year five.

The following numbers come from using the compound interest formula to project your future net worth based on various rates of return. In Chapter 6, we explain how the compound interest formula works in great detail. For now, we'll just jump to the end result. The following table shows how your investments can grow at two modest rates of return. We used a 20 percent and a 25 percent compound rate of return on equity for these examples. The grand total numbers might seem astronomical, especially if you're used to looking at typical rates of return from CDs or stocks or mutual funds. But remember, real estate benefits from leverage, and leverage is what puts real estate investing into a stratosphere by itself. Because of this, fairly modest cash rates of return improve at an exceedingly rapid pace. Here's the idea:

Year	Amount	Years Invested	20% Return	25% Return
1	$ 5,000	25	$ 476,981	$1,323,489
2	$ 5,000	24	$ 397,484	$1,058,791
3	$ 5,000	23	$ 331,237	$ 847,033
4	$ 5,000	22	$ 276,031	$ 677,626
5	$ 5,000	21	$ 230,026	$ 542,101
5	$25,000	21	$ 958,440	$2,168,405
Grand Total			$2,670,199	$6,617,445

Go ahead and pinch yourself, it's OK. Who would have ever thought that by investing in property today you could generate between two to six and a half million dollars in 25 years. What's more, you achieved this by just making one $5,000 investment a year for five years and delayed buying a brand-new car for a while. Yes, of course these numbers are staggering, and, yes, of course it will take work. However, achieving a return like this through investing in real estate is really just a combination of three elements. Big-time real estate investors like Donald Trump are aware of these elements, and now so are you. They are:

1. Leverage

2. Compound interest

3. Time

Is this return on your investment guaranteed? Of course not. But is this type of return from an investment in real estate a very good possibility? Most certainly. In fact, if you get serious about this game it's not only possible, it's probable. What you have to ask yourself is if you want to take your chances on Social Security and your company pension plan being enough. Or do you want to ensure that you'll be in the 5 percent who are financially independent at retirement by making a few small and smart real estate investments now? The decision should be an easy one.

GROUP #2: "TOO BUSY JUST HANGIN' ON"

For baby boomers in the middle of their working lives who are "too busy just hangin' on," life may seem like you're on a runaway train. You're headed down a mountain, don't have any brakes, and God only knows if and when you'll survive it. If you're old enough to remember the Ed Sullivan variety show on television, the host often featured a guest who would spin multiple plates above his head on sticks. This guy had plates spinning above his hands, plates spinning from his feet, and, to top it off, plates spinning from a stick in his mouth. Of course, you see where this story is going: Inevitably, he couldn't keep all the plates spinning and one by one they would each fall and crash to the ground. Sound a little like your life? It's not that you don't make good money; rather, no matter how much you make, there just never seems to be enough to go around. You've got responsibilities: the house, food, kids, clothes, cars, entertainment, soccer camp, music lessons, cleaning, cell phones, cable TV, and on and on.

At this stage in your life you've begun to think about retirement. More accurately, you're beginning to get tired of the daily grind and are secretly wishing for an early retirement. The trouble is you're rightfully concerned about where the money to retire might come from. Maybe your 401(k) or company pension account has taken a hit and you're finally deciding it's time to pay more attention to the future. Great, we've been pitching self-reliance for three chapters now so this is a fine spot to be in. For you, the good news is it's not too late to make a big difference in your retirement picture.

If you followed the numbers in the chart for the "got plenty of time" folks, those same numbers will work for you, too. The difference is that, unlike them, you're not too excited about working for another 25-plus years. If you're in your mid-40s, you've probably been working for 15 or 20 years so far, and you're probably looking at retiring in no more than another 15 or 20 years. However, the reality is that if you don't make some changes right now, you'll be working until you're 65 or 70—not because you want to, but because you need to just to make ends meet. It doesn't have to be that way.

If you understand the story we're telling, you are now well aware of the challenges that lay ahead. Best yet, you want to do something about it. This is good. Unfortunately, because you're on that runaway train doing what you always did, a way out seems like a fading dream. Well, it's not just a dream. Here are a few ideas that if put into practice can make big differences in your life and retirement.

The first principle makes a distinction between wants and needs. These words seem so simple but can be used in enough different ways that they can be confusing. In this society, we seem to be motivated by our wants rather than by the desire to just satisfy our needs. What do we mean? The thought, I want a new BMW, motivates many people to work a little overtime or justify going $50,000 into debt so they can buy one. The fact is that their perfectly good Chevy that's paid for in full does a fine job getting them to and from work every day. Sure a new BMW would be nice, but it won't do anything to help secure a comfortable future for you and your family.

The dilemma gets more complicated as we age and take on new responsibilities. Do we spend $5,000 on a new pool table for the game room or make sure that money is set aside into our kids' college funds? Clearly, the ability to pick the need instead of the want is the biggest initial step in breaking through to a new future. We're sure you realize that most of these decisions in life involve money. If you buy the new BMW instead of driving the paid-for Chevy, your wallet will be that much lighter every month. The truth is, either way, in five years all you'll have is a used car.

If this were just a one-shot decision, we wouldn't be mentioning this concept, but it's not. It's your complete way of thinking about money and spending and saving that has to change. It's about where you shop for almost everything you buy. Do you mow your own lawn for the exercise, or do you pay someone to do it and pay an additional $35 per month to a gym that you don't use? Do you iron your own shirts while watching TV or send them out? Three years of sending your shirts out to be cleaned at $1.25 each costs $937.50. This $937.50 would be the FHA down payment on a $30,000 piece of property. In many parts of the country, $30,000 will buy a decent home. Are you getting the point?

Now try substituting the word "greed" for "want" and the decision becomes one of greed versus need. If you think about all the things you've bought when you spent more than you needed to, you'll probably come to the same conclusion that we have about most items: that is, the wanting brought you more enjoyment than the having.

In fact, for an exercise, conduct a complete financial review of yourself. Write down all the areas each month where you spend money. Many of your expenses will be completely legitimate. Others, however, will strike you as frivolous and a complete waste. The goal is to find areas where you could save by fulfilling needs instead of wants. You don't have to give up all the nice things in life. You just need to sacrifice a little bit now so you can have a lot later.

Ralph Waldo Emerson said, "There is really no insurmountable barrier save your own inherent weakness of purpose." To that end, sell the BMW and pay cash for a used Chevy. Sell the motor home and buy a tent. Iron those shirts, mow the lawn, and get your videos for free at the library. Refinance the house and pull out some money to invest. What we want you to do is substitute needs for wants so you can find the money to invest in your future. It's critical that you give yourself a shot at being in the 5 percent group who will have a comfortable future to look forward to.

In the following table we're going to give you examples of what some small sacrifice might do for you. Again we're using the compound interest formula to arrive at these numbers. We'll use different initial amounts of money and determine where they will take you in the remaining 20 years or so you have left to work. Those of you in this group have a distinct advantage over the younger group we first mentioned. You've worked for 10 or 15 years and have that experience and knowledge when you surmise, "If I were only 25 again and know what I know today." We can't make you 25 again, but instead we just want you to take a deep breath, think long and hard about what you've learned about "doing it the way you always have," and take advantage of capitalism. If you do, you can make yourself and your family some real money—maybe just the kind of money that could make a difference between comfort and squalor in your future.

Amount	Years Invested	20% return	25% return
$ 5,000	20	$ 191,700	$ 433,700
$10,000	20	$ 383,400	$ 867,400
$25,000	20	$ 958,440	$2,168,405
$50,000	20	$1,916,880	$4,336,810

As we said before, with real estate investing these numbers are not only possible but also are probable.

GROUP #3: "WORRIED IT MAY BE TOO LATE"

Personally, we have yet to enter into the "worried it may be too late" group. We do, however, completely understand your concerns for we have helped countless families, friends, and clients like you deal with the financial challenges that go with planning for retirement at your age. Though it may seem like it, it is definitely not too late to make a real difference in your picture. A key advantage for you is you have a world of experience to draw from. Here is a story, a few thoughts, and, finally, our ideas.

In 1954, Ray Kroc, a traveling Multimixer salesman, signed a contract to use the hamburger-selling ideas of the McDonald brothers to open a few places of his own. In his book, *Grinding It Out,* Kroc describes himself as "a battle-scarred veteran of the business wars." He had been working for more than 30 years so far (hadn't graduated from high school) and was battling diabetes and arthritis and the effects of losing his gall bladder and most of his thyroid. At the time he began his burger empire, he was 52 years old. For most of us, 52 is when we want to start slowing down. Starting a business that we knew nothing about wouldn't even enter our minds. Nonetheless, for Ray Kroc the rest was history. By 1976 McDonald's would surpass $1 billion in total revenue. It took IBM and Xerox 46 years and 63 years, respectively, to reach that mark.

We're not suggesting you become a hamburger mogul, but we do want you to realize what is possible for those on the latter end of their working lives. Kroc's story is incredible—you probably won't duplicate it. What we want is for you to seize the opportunity America has to offer so you can live the happy ending to your story. In the words of a French proverb, "To believe a thing impossible is to make it so."

We began this section with some words about risk and excessive caution. In all likelihood, if you're not comfortable now, it's probably because you didn't take a couple of chances at success when you were younger. Alternatively, perhaps you did take some chances, but for one reason or another they just didn't work out. Our ideas and this book are meant to give you some concrete ways to give it another try. Helen Keller said, "When one door of opportunity closes, another opens; but often we look so long at the closed door that we do not see the one which has opened for us."

At this stage of your life, having clear-cut financial goals is of paramount importance. For you, it will be somewhat easier to complete the charts we provided earlier because you're already staring retirement in the eye. Remember that statistically your life span is getting longer every year. If you're 55 years old, your life expectancy is 79.1 for men and 83.2 for women. At 65, it jumps to 81.6 for men and 84.9 for women. That's a long time to be alive with no job to go to and no money to help you enjoy your free time.

For anyone in this category, your most important goal will be to focus on creating spendable income that is hedged against inflation. You definitely should have some reserves in the bank for emergencies, but because of the effects of inflation, savings-type investments tend to have diminishing value. In fact, the rates of return these types of investments pay after taxes are usually just about at the rate of inflation. So if you spend the interest income, the purchasing power of the savings nest egg decreases each year. We believe that the best place to find inflation-hedging cash flow is from owning rental property. Most of the remainder of this book will be dedicated to helping you understand how to take full advantage of this kind of investment.

If you're in this third group, the real secret to being successful will come from a change in your focus. The strategies we laid out for the first two groups were centered on overcoming shortfalls in the nest egg and building toward dreams for an eventual retirement. Instead of long-term wealth building, this third group has to focus directly on creating cash flow now to live day to day. At this point it's not about the percentage return that's important; it's an actual monthly cash return that needs to be your real focal point.

As mentioned, if your retirement is imminent, then your primary focus will be finding the property or properties that will give you the highest monthly cash return. The best way to achieve this goal is to either pay all cash for a building or, alternatively, put down at least a sizable amount of money to minimize any mortgage payment. However, if you can work at least ten more years, you still have the time to take advantage of some amount of leverage. Your goal will be to find one or more properties that will provide you with the greatest cash flow at that retirement point. Because the most conservative goal is to have that property paid off by the time you retire, let's work toward that end.

An ideal property would be one with an assumable loan that would be fully amortized (paid off) the month you retire. It would be even better if the down payment were exactly the same as your investment nest egg. We know this doesn't always happen, so here are a few ideas that can help you get close:

1. We have found that most mortgages that are at least ten years pay off principal at a fairly rapid clip. Also, by making an additional principal payment each month, most of these loans can be paid off in about half the time as the current payoff date. In many cases, any cash flow from the property could be enough to help accomplish that task. The more you focus on sound management, the faster you can get that loan paid off.

2. If you can't find a property you can pay off on its own merits, you may have to help it along when you retire. It may not work out for you to live in your rental building, so one solution might be to sell the big house and buy a smaller property in a retirement area. You can use some of the extra proceeds from the sale to pay off the balance of the mortgage or reduce it enough so you can get it paid off very soon after retirement.

3. If you are in a limited down payment situation, you may have to count on leverage more than we have been talking

about. Leverage can produce some huge equity gains over a number of years, but more risk is involved than with the conservative steps we've been discussing. This may be warranted, considering the gloomy future of ending up in the 95 percentile group we keep talking about. So you follow a five- to ten-year growth-oriented program to build the biggest nest egg you can. The goal will be to sell at retirement and move that money into high-cash-flow nonleveraged property. You will have to pay some taxes to accomplish the goal, but planning with your certified public accountant (CPA) or tax expert can minimize that.

Finally, we want to try to debunk the myth of the "free-and-clear" house. Burning that mortgage is probably one of the major goals most of us have after paying on that property for 20 to 30 years. While it might be great to have the place paid off, that house is really the largest wasted asset most of us will possess in our lifetime. This is because the large equity you have in it, though it does provide you with a warm fuzzy feeling all over, doesn't produce any spendable income for you. We're well aware that to suggest that you sell the family home is about as popular as burning the flag. You may not need to sell it to improve your lifestyle, but you do need to start thinking about it as an asset, not just as your home. Here are a few ideas that should help.

For starters, if you were game and didn't need as much room anymore, selling your home would be by far the smartest business move you could make. With tax laws as they exist today, there would be no capital gain on the profit for selling your home up to $250,000 if you're single, or up to $500,000 if you're married. This could be a tremendous way to create a retirement nest egg out of nothing. The good news is that you can use this tax rule to your advantage over and over again as long as you follow the rules.

If, however, you are committed to keeping your house (and it is perfectly OK if you are), you should look into refinancing it to generate the cash necessary to invest in income property. At this point, if you've had your loan for many years, a large portion of your payment is probably going toward paying off the loan. This is called principal reduction. In most cases you can take out a new loan and keep your payment close to the same as it currently is. A move like this should net you enough cash to make a nice investment in a rental property. And a rental property with a decent-size down payment could bring you a nice monthly income. The idea is to keep your house payment the same and create an increased cash flow from the property you purchase.

Another added attraction is that your tax benefits from your home will increase, because the interest part of your payment will now be higher. Remember, you can't deduct the portion of your payment that goes toward principal, only the interest portion.

The table that follows may give you some examples of the kind of cash flow you might expect from the funds you take out of your home. The percentages are the cash-on-cash return from the amount invested in the property. The amount invested is the down payment, which is the number on the left-hand side of the chart. The dollar figure under the percentages is the estimated annual cash flow.

| | Estimated Annual Cash Flow | | |
Amount Invested	10%	15%	20%
$ 25,000	$ 2,500	$ 3,750	$ 5,000
$ 50,000	$ 5,000	$ 7,500	$10,000
$100,000	$10,000	$15,000	$20,000
$150,000	$15,000	$22,500	$30,000

For most of us who ended up with a larger home for the family, this extra space really isn't needed once the kids leave home. The most practical move for parents without kids in the house anymore is to find a smaller, more economical place to live. In most areas, small to medium-size investment properties include very nice owners' units. With a reasonable down payment, these properties can provide a nice place to live for a minimum monthly cost. Better yet, based on your down payment, they may even provide a free place to live plus some positive cash flow.

For those of you who don't own yet, it's time to get busy and buy some small units. Many programs are available that will allow you to buy a piece of property with little or no down payment. We recommend you buy a small set of rental units, something with two, three, or four units. This way you will have the best chance of a controllable cost of living that can decrease as you raise rents over the years. There are also some tax benefits and equity growth from appreciation and loan payoff.

If you've avoided the problems of ownership so far in your life, just remember what the future holds for those not brave enough to work their way out of the 95 percentile group. Life is full of problems, and many people choose to spend all the money they make at work to take full advantage of enjoying life today. This approach to life can work fine as long as you are capable of working forever. Unfortunately, none of us are Superman and we'll all have to retire one day. Sadly, our retirement system is set up to allow you to only scrape by, at best.

The other issue is natural conservatism, which we all seem to gravitate toward as we get older. It's an offshoot of losing that invincibility of youth. We've learned the hard way that things don't always work out as we wanted or planned. What's more, some of those hard lessons cost us dearly. From a financial point of view we frequently hear the following, "I don't want to take any chances with what I have because I'm too old" or "I don't have the ability to make the money back." In principle we agree. But as a wise woman once said, "Take risks. You can't fall off the bottom."

Even though investing in your future means taking a risk, isn't that 95 percentile statistic more like a guarantee of a miserable life during your waning years? We're not suggesting you risk all your savings on a long shot at the racetrack or buy lottery tickets. We're suggesting you dedicate some of your energies and money to beginning a new chapter in your life. If you do your homework, it will be very rewarding financially. Equally important, it may give you a new interest in life and something to do when you've got the gold watch and the boot from your day job.

CHAPTER 4

THE APPRECIATION GAME

"What one man can do, another can do."
—SIR ANTHONY HOPKINS IN "THE EDGE"

We began this book at the end of the story, that is, where you might be when it comes time to retire. We did so to emphasize what might happen if you wait much longer to examine this issue. We hope you see that you really shouldn't wait any longer to get started. Yes, we know how tough it is to compete in today's world. Things are moving so fast that it almost seems impossible to take a deep breath and learn something new. But you have to start sometime.

Again, there are no guarantees. As with any type of investment, you earn a return because there is some element of risk. You can put $10,000 under your mattress, but you won't earn any profit because you are supposedly taking the risk out of the equation. But are you really? Your house could burn down or you could get robbed. You get the point: Your money isn't safe even under a mattress.

Real estate, though, is historically one of the safest investments you can make, because it is a tangible asset and one in which you can become the captain of your own ship. Nonetheless, ungrounded fear of losing their money keeps most people from ever getting started. We have, however, tried to turn the tables on you. We've told you what will likely happen if you don't invest. Not a pretty picture. Nonetheless, the outlook for those who are on board is bright. To that end, let's look at some property and play the Appreciation Game.

REAL-LIFE EXAMPLE PROPERTY IN 2002

Figure 4.1 shows the financial breakdown of a real property that we will use throughout the rest of the book as an example. It consists of two houses on one lot in Lawndale, California. Lawndale is in the South Bay area of Los Angeles and is a microcosm of demographics for most communities. It is an entry-level city for home ownership and first-time investors. Note that these are actual numbers from a real property taken from the Greater South Bay Regional Multiple Listing Service in 2002.

REAL-LIFE COMPARABLE PROPERTY SALE FROM 1977

Now that you see the financial parameters of the example property, what follows is the actual information from the sale of a comparable duplex from the same neighborhood (just six blocks away) from 1977 (See Figure 4.2). We'll look at what happened to the value of these properties when we examine them in a 25-year time span. The idea now is to illustrate what the Appreciation Game is really all about.

This is a real-life picture of what investing in this property would mean today for the person who bought it in 1977. For our 1977 investor, the property that cost $59,000 25 years ago has a market value today of $279,000. That is an increase in value of

FIGURE 4.1
EXAMPLE PROPERTY

Property
    Address: 4056 West 165th Street
        Lawndale, California
    Number of Units: 2 houses on 1 lot
    Unit Mix: 1 × 2 bedroom, 1 × 1 bedroom
    Year Built: 1948

Property Financial Parameters
    Purchase Price: $279,000
    Monthly Income $ 2,250
    (2 bdrm, $1,250; 1 bdrm, $1,000):
    Equity: $ 8,370
    Monthly Expenses: $ 448

Existing Encumbrances
    First Trust Deed Amount: $270,630
    Interest Rate: 7.0%
    Years of Loan: 30
    Monthly Payment: $ 1,801

Miscellaneous Parameters
    Appreciation Rate: 5.0%
    Vacancy Rate: 2.5%
    Land Value: $ 83,370
    Depreciable Improvements: $195,300

Expense Detail
    Property Taxes: $ 3,348
    Licenses: $ 30
    Management: $ 423
    Insurance Costs: $ 541
    Utilities: $ 423
    Maintenance: $ 317
    Miscellaneous Expenses: $ 294
    Total Expenses: $ 5,376

FIGURE 4.2
COMPARABLE PROPERTY SALE FROM 1977

Property

Address:	4032 West 159th Street
	Lawndale, California
Number of Units:	2 houses on 1 lot
Unit Mix:	1 × 2 bedroom, 1 × 1 bedroom
Year Built:	1947

Property Financial Parameters

Purchase Price:	$59,000
Monthly Income	$ 425
(2 bdrm, $250; 1 bdrm, $175):	
Equity:	$ 1,770
Monthly Expenses:	$ 85

Existing Encumbrances

First Trust Deed Amount:	$57,230
Interest Rate:	7.0%
Years of Loan:	30
Monthly Payment:	$ 381

Miscellaneous Parameters

Appreciation Rate:	6.5%
Vacancy Rate:	2.5%
Land Value:	$17,700
Depreciable Improvements:	$41,300

Expense Detail

Property Taxes:	$ 708
Licenses:	$ 0
Management:	$ 60
Insurance Costs:	$ 108
Utilities:	$ 60
Maintenance:	$ 36
Miscellaneous Expenses:	$ 48
Total Expenses:	$ 1,020

$220,000. Note that these numbers weren't made up; they are based on actual sales that took place between comparable properties in this average community in 1977 and again in 2002.

Assuming you bought that duplex in 1977, we can make some calculations and project what the financial summary for this property would look like today. To that end, we'll factor in an increase in income of 3.5 percent per year and an increase of the expenses of 2.5 percent per year. We'll also use 6.5 percent as the appreciation rate and add in a vacancy factor of 2.5 percent. Given these parameters, the outlook in 2002 for this property would be:

Market Value	$279,000
Loan Balances	$ 19,500
Equity Position	$259,500
Account Balance	$ 41,000

Besides the fantastic value appreciation that took place, this projection shows that the investor has generated in excess of $40,000 in positive cash flow and tax benefits while owning this property.

For the balance of our discussions we will assume that our conservative investor used some of this excess to completely pay off the mortgage. The first impact of this free-and-clear property is the way it affects our conservative investor's balance sheet. This is a property worth $279,000—that's more than a quarter of a million dollars. According to the July 2002 issue of *Money* magazine, this one asset alone puts our investor near the top in all categories of net worth (see Figure 4.3); not bad considering this could have been accomplished with as little as $1,800 down using an FHA loan 25 years ago.

The more important number for a conservative, retirement-oriented investor is how this type of investment creates a significant monthly income stream. To project what kind of cash flow could be created with an investment like this, we know that the two-bedroom unit in our example property rents for $1,250 per

FIGURE 4.3

APPROXIMATE Net WORTH BY INCOME

Income	Approximate Net Worth
Under $25,000	$ 7,550
$25,000 – $49,999	$ 34,600
$50,000 – $74,999	$ 53,375
$75,000 – $99,999	$ 80,073
$100,000 – $124,999	$145,203
$125,000 – $149,999	$214,182
$150,000 and up	$357,091

Source: National Market Audit, weighted, Claritas 2001.

month, and that the one-bedroom unit rents for $1,000. The taxes will be calculated at today's rates. Insurance and utilities will be estimated based on the current market. Given these parameters, the following chart gives an estimate of the cash flow that this property might generate today:

Income	$2,250
Expenses	
Taxes	$ 250
Insurance	$ 50
Utilities	$ 60
Maintenance	$ 112
Vacancy	$ 68
Total	$ 540
Net Cash Flow	$1,710

As we're sure you would agree, this estimated monthly net income of $1,710 would certainly help create a nice retirement cushion.

Of course, our investor's $1,710 positive cash flow per month is no fortune by any stretch of the imagination, but combined with other retirement income the fruits of this $1,800 investment from 25 years ago are obvious. Additionally, this income is a hedge against inflation, for this property owner can pass any inflationary increase along to his or her renters by gradually raising the rents over the years.

Besides cash flow, which is great to have, we want to show you where you might be in the future from a nest-egg position, assuming you bought a property like this today. To calculate such a projection, we must know how much the property will appreciate over the next 25 years. Although we can't be sure, the past is a prologue and can reasonably be used to make an estimate.

Our example property increased in value from $59,000 in 1977 to $279,000 in 2002. That increase of $220,000 represents an annual increase in value of 6.41 percent. We'll use the same parameters as we used before, but to be ultraconservative we will lower the appreciation rate from 6.5 percent to just 5 percent. Even so, here is how that property value will look 25 years down the road:

Market Value	$960,539 (1)
Loan Balance	$ 97,446 (2)
Equity Position	$863,092
Account Balance	$237,529 (3)

Had you bought the building in 2002 and kept it for 25 years, here is a summary of how you would make out:

Value in 2027	$960,539 (Number 1 above)
Loan Balance	$ 97,446 (Number 2 above)
Account Balance	$237,529 (Number 3 above)
Monthly Income	$ 5,317
Expenses	$ 835
Net Monthly Income	$ 4,482

Finally, in the following chart we have added a rate of 3 percent to account for inflation (for those of you who are mathematically inclined, this is called the "discounted present value"). With this adjustment, you will now be able to see the true future benefit of an investment like this in today's dollars:

Inflation-Adjusted Values

	2027	Adjusted
Property Value	$960,539	$450,000
Net Monthly Income	$ 4,482	$ 2,140

As you can see, a future monthly cash flow of $4,482 (or an inflation-adjusted cash flow of $2,140) on a small real estate investment today isn't something to scoff at. No doubt these numbers are based on a lot of assumptions. But establishing future expected returns from all investments is based on making some kind of assumptions. In this case, we were as conservative as possible by basing our projections on the actual historical data for a typical, specific property in a typical, specific place. We did this so you could see what really happened.

PROOF IN THE PUDDING

You're probably asking yourself, "Does analyzing a duplex in Lawndale, California, do anything for my future?" The answer is yes, but just to be sure, we want you to see that this type of cash flow and asset appreciation are not atypical. We realize that the California economy this example came from may not be totally representative of other areas of the country. For that reason we asked Realtors in a couple other areas to help us show the long-term benefits in their locales. These numbers vary, but the bottom line is that a real estate investment, regardless of area, offers an opportunity to acquire an appreciating asset. The only hitch is that you stay in the game for a while.

Our first example is a two-unit property located in the metropolitan area of Denver, Colorado. Here are its basic financial parameters, including the price fetched in its most recent sale as well as a sale from 22 years ago:

Address:	3653 West 89th Way
	Denver, Colorado
Age:	Built in 1972
Unit Mix:	2 × 2 bedroom/1 bath units
Size:	1,865 square feet
	Approximately 930 square feet each
2001 Value:	$271,000
1979 Value:	$ 78,500

Value appreciation rate data courtesy of Kathy Schuler at Prestige Realty in Inglewood, Co.

The next example is another two-unit building. This one is located in Winthrop, Massachusetts, just outside of Boston:

Address:	76-78 Crystal Cove
	Winthrop, Massachusetts
Age:	Built in 1870
Unit Mix:	2 × 5 bedroom/2 bath units
Size:	4,740 square feet
	Approximately 2,370 square feet each
2002 Value:	$399,000 (adjusted price)
1980 Value:	$53,000

Value appreciation rate data courtesy of James H. Man at Marr Real Estate in Winthrop, MA.

Finally, the last property is also a two-unit building, located in Port Huron, Michigan:

Address:	2856 East Rick Drive
	Port Huron, Michigan
Age:	Built in 1970
Unit Mix:	2 × 2 bedroom/1 bath units

Size: 1,664 square feet
                         Approximately 830 square feet each
2002 Value: $100,000
1985 Value: $44,500

Value appreciation rate data courtesy of Larry Lick at Rental Housing Online (rhol.org) in Port Huron, MI.

The following chart summarizes the appreciation that took place on each of the four properties just described.

Location of Property	Time Span between Sales	Appreciation Rate
Lawndale, CA	25	6.41%
Denver, CO	22	5.53%
Winthrop, MA	22	9.61%
Port Huron, MI	17	4.88%

Although this is a very limited sample compared to the vast number of properties in the country, it is certainly not unusual. Real estate generally appreciates over time, and these real-life examples from all over the country prove it. It is this appreciation that allows you to grow a small sum of money into a significant retirement asset. What is even better is that as the value of the real estate asset grows, so does the income stream it generates, and you can then use that income stream to pay off the mortgage. When you retire, you will have a mortgage-free stream of steady income. And when the time is right, you can increase that income stream by raising rents. No market turnaround is necessary, no Federal Reserve Board chairman pronouncements to the contrary.

So by jumping into this game and buying even a few units, you can avoid being part of the 95 percentile who retire practically broke and can instead create that retirement income we've been talking about. You will be able to get the mortgage paid off in 25 years. You will create a steady retirement cash flow. You will secure a fruitful future for you and your family. All this for a small investment today.

Why is real estate such a smart retirement investment? Perhaps Mark Twain understood the Appreciation Game better than anyone when he declared, "Buy land, they ain't making it anymore."

YOUR YELLOW BRICK ROAD

Now that you are aware of how appreciation really works, let's lay the groundwork for making it happen for you.

There is no way any of us can become experts on all the areas of life that affect us, but on the really important issues, the ones that hit us in the pocketbook, it is incumbent that we develop a good basic understanding of how they work. Here's a simple question: How many of us have an incredible base of knowledge about sports or our favorite movie star's life but don't know what the LIBOR is? Exactly. (LIBOR is the London Interbank Offered Rate.)

We aren't poking fun at anyone for having fun; actually, being able to enjoy life to the fullest is one of the biggest benefits to finally taking charge of your future. What we have seen is that most of us tend to abdicate all responsibility for our future to the professionals we hire to help us. Not unlike an ostrich who buries his head in the sand at the first sign of trouble. Of course you need an educated stockbroker to help pick the right stocks, or a trained real estate professional to help choose which property to buy. But wouldn't it be nice if you had a keen understanding of either of those fields before you hired someone else to run the ship?

We also know that most of us are impatient. Once we read a book on this—or take a course on that—and the lightbulb goes on, well, we can't wait to get started. We say, "Wait." People have and will continue to make fortunes investing in all kinds of investments, including real estate, for as long as time goes on. Opportunities to make money are not going to go away. We say be patient. Take the time to gain the basic knowledge necessary so you can make sound decisions on what to invest in and who to turn to for help. Remember, investing doesn't guarantee a return, but knowledge certainly helps make the odds much more attractive.

The Declaration of Independence says, "We hold these truths to be self-evident . . ." Well, we hold the following truth to be self-evident, too: You can educate yourself, utilize some sound business principles, and then implement an ultraconservative investment plan and take much of the risk out of real estate investing while still allowing for a sizable return on your investment. In the end you'll have created a yellow brick road to your own retirement. If you're interested, we have a plan to help.

THE FIVE-POINT PLAN

Our plan is fairly simple and designed to keep you in the game for as long as you have your money invested. This isn't meant to be a course called "Real Estate Investing 101" that you take once and forget. This is more like a continuing education class—one that you should be involved in for the rest of your investment career. Just as you educated yourself for that day job, we want you to educate yourself for this investment career. You work at your day job and trade your time for dollars. In your investment career you will be letting your investments do most of the work, but you need to be the brains of the operation. Yes, you will be hiring some experts to help, but it takes knowledge to hire the right people.

The five key steps of our plan for success are:

1. Learn

2. Research

3. Plan

4. Invest

5. Manage

Let's touch on each of these components of the plan.

STEP ONE: LEARN

The first step, learning, can be the toughest for most of us, because learning anything new requires lots of personal effort. When it comes to full-time careers, if you wanted to be an engineer you would go to college and get a degree in engineering. But don't worry, a formal education is not necessary for you to learn what you need to learn in order to succeed in real estate investing.

Thankfully, thousands of books, newspaper articles, classes, seminars, and tapes are available on most investment subjects. Even better news is that most of the books, articles, and some of the tapes probably will be available for free at your local library. To supplement your independent study, plenty of colleges and adult education schools offer courses on everything from basic accounting to property management. Most are truly informative and reasonably priced.

For the majority of us, finding the time to devote to a new venture is one of the toughest problems we face. We have found that many audio programs are available on a host of investment subjects, not just real estate. They can be tougher to locate but are worth the effort. You can literally turn your daily commute into an education effort by using the time to listen to these audio educational programs rather than talk radio or music. It would be a trade-off, but one that could get you that much closer to catching the golden goose.

Finally, as of June 2002, the Amazon.com Web site lists 5,122 books on real estate, more than enough to make you an expert on the subject. Now, we're not suggesting that you read all these books before you buy a property; this is just to illustrate how much help is available.

STEP TWO: RESEARCH

In step two, research, you put the knowledge you have gained in the first step to work. Like test-driving a car before you buy, you will begin using what you've learned about your investment vehicle in the real world. In real estate you will learn about capitalization rates, gross multipliers, and the price per square foot as ways of comparing properties. These rates can vary greatly even in the same city. Once you understand these concepts and their importance, you can begin to get a feeling for the statistics on the properties in your area.

You can actually begin the research phase of this plan while you are learning in step one. You don't need a four-year college education to be able to get a gut-level feeling about the products you're researching. Just as you can research various no-load mutual funds that are growth oiented, you can discover what duplexes are selling for in your neighborhood. What you learn in step one you apply in step two. During this process you should also begin to research the experts in the field so you will ultimately find the professionals you will feel comfortable with and have confidence in. Feel free to meet real estate agents and loan brokers. Interview them as if you're considering hiring them for a job—because you are.

A word of warning is important here. Did you ever hear the phrase, "A little knowledge is a dangerous thing"? Well, by this point in time you will have a little knowledge, and it will indeed be a dangerous thing. By diving in the way you might and doing the kind of research we're recommending, you will probably be pretty enthusiastic about getting started. You will start seeing "good deals" out there and be tempted to jump in and get started right away. But put the brakes on. Wait at least until you complete step three in this process, the planning phase; this way you will have a self-written road map to help guide you toward your dreams.

STEP THREE: PLAN

Planning is the key to being successful in any business. Certainly, knowledge and research are important, but if you strike out spending your money on the wrong products, you may not reach your goals. A great buy on a duplex that produces no cash flow does little for a retired investor who needs income.

In Chapter 6, we will be reviewing planning in detail. But in short, a good plan starts with defining what your goals are. Your goal cannot be to find a "good deal." When it comes to investing, everyone's goal is to find one of those; that's a given in the field. When you tell your real estate agent that you're looking for a "good deal," it lets him or her know how little you really are in touch with your true needs.

The exercise in Chapter 2 to determine your lump-sum gap and the amount to fund your dreams was designed to help you focus on measurable goals from your investments. These should be the things you truly want for you and your family. These become flags on your financial road map to keep you on course to reaching your goals. It is chasing the truly important personal things that make life a wonderful experience. Don't get caught at the end of your life realizing you were using someone else's map.

STEP FOUR: INVEST

The fourth step in our plan is where you make your move. This is when you get to put that knowledge and research to work by investing and buying your first property. This is where the real work starts, because it's not just a mind game now, it's for real.

When you've finally decided it's time to buy something, take a deep breath and review all you've learned and researched before you make that first purchase. This can be as exciting as buying your first car or home, so the deep breath will save you from jumping for the first property that seems to be "exactly" what you want. Remember what Will Rogers said: "Don't just grab the first thing that comes by, know what to turn down."

When you get to the point of actually making an investment, the process can take a while. This is especially true when purchasing a piece of real estate. But if that looking-around time seems to go on way too long, you may have to reassess the standards and goals in your plan. Remember, you can analyze, research, and plan on paper until you're blue in the face, but it's impossible to make a profit investing in real estate if you don't actually make an investment. What's more, it's pretty easy in the textbook world of learning and research to be out of step with the real world. Make sure you ask your expert to let you know if your goals are out of line with the current market. In the end, make a purchase and get started.

Owning property is like going to work after you are finished with school. We all have heard the story of the person who started in the mail room and ended up running the entire company. Well, in real estate you don't have to start out with a 20-unit building to be successful. You can start small, too, in the "mail room" of real estate investments. How about starting with a modest duplex close to where you live? Or, better yet, if you don't own a home yet, buy a duplex and live in one of the units. That's what we call starting in the mail room of the real estate business. It is a nice, safe, conservative approach.

STEP FIVE: MANAGE

When you own property, you have the full responsibility of running it. However, just as surgeons don't perform operations before they are properly trained, neither should you invest even a penny until you are trained, too. Chapter 10 is devoted to this topic, but let's hit some highlights now.

Once you are trained, the good news is that you will own the property, and you can do as much or as little of the work as you like. You are in charge of the property, the rents, and the tenants. In good times you can hire out most of the work, and in the tough times you can do it yourself. You are in control. You have to work at it and assume the responsibility, but that's what makes it safe for you.

You've got a day job that you call a career, but you're just trading time for dollars there. Now, whether you've hung a shingle or not, you are heading up your own real estate company as the CEO and CFO all rolled into one. You're now in charge of investing your hard-earned money, and the success of this operation depends solely on you and how well you do the job. This is frightening, but liberating, at the same time.

Take another deep breath; remember, you've conducted your research, you've studied the market, and you've planned where you're going. As we've said before, this isn't a get-rich-quick program. You are on a life journey. The plan is to invest your money to grow your net worth to meet the goals you have set for you and your family.

You will find that if you are doing your job right as the manager, you will be constantly revisiting the first four steps of the plan for success. As you manage, you learn—not from books this time but from actually doing the job. Running a property is really an on-the-job research project. You'll become quite an expert as you handle the day-to-day operations of your property.

Along the way you will take the time to assess the current market and compare your position with the goals of your plan. At some point as head of this company, you will decide that it's time to trade up or refinance. Either way, you may realize that the time is ripe to acquire more property and you are going to use your previously owned buildings to help you do it. When this happens, it's back to step four, for you'll have a new property to manage. The fun is just beginning!

CHAPTER 5

COMPONENTS
OF RETURN

"Money is better than poverty, if only for financial reasons."
–WOODY ALLEN

W hen investing in residential real estate, these components of return will help you reach your goals:

1. Cash flow

2. Loan reduction

3. Appreciation

4. Tax benefits

To take full advantage of real estate as an investment, all four components of return must be factored into the equation. In this chapter you will learn about each component independently and then how to calculate the combined effect of each of them to produce an anticipated overall return on your investment.

This information will help you see the trees through the forest. At the outset it will show you what kind of profit you can achieve on any potential investment, and, second, it will give you a yardstick against which to measure all properties you might be considering. The idea is to compare prospective purchases on a level playing field. Once this is achieved, the decision on which one to actually buy should become relatively simple.

To help demonstrate each component of return, we will use the example duplex we introduced in Chapter 4, "The Appreciation Game."

CASH FLOW

The first component of return, and the one that usually gets the most attention from novice investors, is cash flow. In simple terms, cash flow is the money you get to keep after all the expenses have been paid. The misnomer made by many beginning investors is that cash flow is the component of return that helps you grow wealthy. True, it's nice to be on the positive side of the line at the end of each month, but when it comes to true wealth building, it's the other components that really do the trick.

Nonetheless, to determine cash flow, you need to know the following:

1. The annual gross income

2. The annual expenses

3. The total debt payment on your loans

THE INCOME

There are three ways to look at the income a building produces. The first way is by examining the scheduled rent. Scheduled rent is the sum total of all the established rents for the building. This analysis assumes that each tenant is paying in full and that there are no vacancies.

The second way to look at the income is by analyzing the potential rent. Potential rent is that income you can earn if you were charging market rent for your building. This analysis is based on the rents that other property owners in your neighborhood are receiving. This is where any ongoing rental income research you do can have a major impact on your cash flow and, in later years, on the ultimate value of your property.

The most effective way to analyze the income on a building is to look at the collected rent. A collected rent analysis is like swearing before a judge; it tells the truth, the whole truth, and nothing but the truth. This analysis tells what money was actually taken in over a period of time. It combines the rent that was collected, as well as the rent that was not, plus adding in the true cost for any vacancies that occurred.

Note that the credit losses you endure from bad debts will depend on a few things: the general state of the economy, the economic level of your tenant base, and most important, your adeptness as an effective property manager. Remember, however, credit losses from occasional vacancies are par for the course in this business and come with the territory. In the very best scenario, your vacancies would only be "turnovers" (a change of tenants with no lost rent). This goal often can be achieved but will require hands-on management on your part.

THE EXPENSES

Expenses are the second factor in determining cash flow on a piece of real estate. There are three different types of expenses: fixed expenses, variable expenses, and capital expenses.

Fixed expenses are the commonplace recurring costs required when holding a property, including insurance premiums, property taxes, and city business license fees. They are called fixed expenses because the amount you pay on a regular basis does not change.

Variable expenses, on the other hand, do change. These expenses are all the other costs you may incur while managing your rental property, including general upkeep, maintenance, and utility payments. Obviously, the effective management of variable expenses will play a pivotal role in how much cash flow a building produces.

The last type of expense is capital expenses. Capital expenses are defined as major items that have a useful life of more than one year, like a new driveway, new roof, or exterior paint. For tax purposes, these items must be capitalized, or written off, over a period of years. To account for capital expenses in your cash flow, you will need to include a reserve of a certain percentage of the income based on the condition of the property.

Now we'll calculate cash flow for our example property: Here we have two units that rent for a total of $2,250 per month. Multiply $2,250 by 12 months and the gross scheduled income on the property is $27,000 per year. Furthermore, the actual annual expenses add up to $5,376 and the loan payment is $1,801 per month, which is $21,612 yearly. Because we put down $8,370 to buy the property with a 3 percent down FHA loan, we can compute our cash flow return as follows:

Gross Annual Income	$27,000
Less Operating Expenses	– $ 5,376
Less Annual Loan Payments	– $21,612
Annual Cash Flow	$ 12

Then, to determine the percentage return on your investment, divide the cash flow by the down payment:

Annual cash flow $12 ÷ Down payment $8,370
= Less than 1 percent return

As you can see, with the 3 percent that we put down in our example, this property didn't produce a very good cash-on-cash return. But remember, our goal wasn't cash-on-cash return. If it were, we would have made a much more significant down payment. Rather, our goal was to start investing now to ensure a cash flow for retirement. To that end, we are assuming you are using an extremely low down payment to get started.

LOAN REDUCTION

Loan reduction is the second way your equity will grow over the tenure of your purchase. When you close on a piece of real estate, your initial equity is your down payment. Thankfully, with the help of your tenants, your equity will dramatically increase over the years. This is because you are making monthly payments on your mortgage using tenant income. In the first few years of ownership, it's difficult to notice loan reduction as much of a return because so much of your payment is going toward interest. But in latter years, your monthly mortgage payments pay down principal at a rapid rate, which significantly increases your equity.

To illustrate equity growth from loan reduction, let's return to our two-unit example property. To recap, we financed a $270,630 loan that was payable at $1,801 per month. The payment included interest at 7 percent per year as well as principal reduction. The total payments on the loan for the year are $21,612. Given these facts, we can compute our equity growth returns in the first year as follows:

Total Loan Payments	$21,612
Less Interest Paid	–$18,944
Principal Reduction	$ 2,668

Principal reduction $2,668 ÷ Down
payment $8,370 = 31.8% Return

APPRECIATION

The third way your equity grows is through value appreciation. Value appreciation results from two factors, inflation and demand. Inflationary appreciation sounds like just what it is—the increase in a piece of real estate's value caused by inflation. This appreciation rate is directly linked to the general inflationary rate of the country's overall economy. When the country's inflation rate is up, the appreciation rate of property usually is also up.

Demand is the second factor connected to appreciation. Demand appreciation is related to four economic principles. They are:

1. Scarcity

2. Transferability

3. Utility

4. Demand

These four components can affect a property's appreciation rate in varying degrees. It is the combined effect of these principles that pushes property values up at a greater rate in some areas while pushing values down in others.

The scarcity principle can best be seen when comparing an urban area to a rural one. In urban areas, it is nearly impossible to find any undeveloped land. Just think of New York City or downtown Chicago and you'll get the picture. In cities like these, to build a new building an existing older building must be bulldozed. Therefore, you first must find someone willing to sell. Once that is accomplished, you'll most definitely be paying a premium for both the land and the existing structure that sits on it. Naturally, this drives prices up. Rural areas, on the other hand, tend to have plenty of vacant land available. This greater availability of land makes it pretty simple to find willing sellers; the end result is lower prices for real estate in these areas.

Transferability refers to the ease of buying and selling any commodity. As you know, investments such as stocks and bonds are fairly liquid because you can transfer them from one owner to another pretty quickly. Real estate, on the other hand, can't trade hands nearly so fast. This is usually related to the number of potential buyers and the ability, or lack thereof, to find adequate financing. There may be many buyers and hundreds of lenders for the modest two-bedroom/one bath home you are trying to sell, but how many buyers and lenders would be interested or qualified to buy the Chrysler Building? Significantly fewer.

Utility refers to the usability of property. With real estate, the value of a property is directly related to its highest and best use. For example, a small parcel of land in a residential area will probably be limited by the potential value of the home that can be built on it. A large commercial lot close to a highway entrance or a shipyard, however, could be an extremely valuable location to build a manufacturing plant. According to this principle, the greater the utility value, the greater the price of the property.

Finally, the demand principle of appreciation results from the upward desirability of the property. This is the same phenomenon that affects the price of tickets to any major event that sells out at a moment's notice. Think about the scalpers that roam the parking lot of the Super Bowl or a Bruce Springsteen concert, for example; the reason they are able to get top dollar for their tickets is because the demand for their product is so great. If these scalpers were hawking tickets to see a clown making balloon animals, odds are they wouldn't attract many top-dollar buyers.

General trends in the economy also play a significant role in changes in demand. Many investors move from one investment vehicle to another based on the investment's ability to produce a buck. When stocks are up, their money is there. When bond yields increase, the stocks are sold for bonds. When real estate is moving, they start buying. This sends the message to all the small investors that it is time to buy. The end result is an increased demand for a product that is in limited supply. In times like these, appreciation rates naturally increase.

To give an example of how appreciation affects price, let's make an estimate using our example property. Remember, we bought the example property for $279,000. We'll assume the appreciation rate is 5 percent per year. At that price, and with that appreciation rate, the return looks like this:

Price of Property	$279,000
Appreciation Rate	× 5%
Total Return	$ 13,950

We can calculate the percentage return for the first year of ownership by dividing the appreciation by the down payment:

Appreciation $13,950 ÷ Down payment $8,370 = 166% Return

Yes, a 166 percent return isn't half bad. Remember, we put only 3 percent of the purchase price down to purchase this property and the bank financed the balance. Therefore, leverage was the reason we achieved such a phenomenal result. As you can see, this modest appreciation rate of just 5 percent translated into a tremendous return on our investment.

TAX BENEFITS

The fourth and final component of return is tax-sheltered benefits. These benefits are the paper losses you can deduct from the taxable income you receive from the property. Because you are the owner of an investment property, the Internal Revenue Service allots you an annual depreciation allowance to deduct against your income. The premise is that this deduction will be saved up and used to replace the property at the end of its useful life. For most businesses, this is a necessary deduction because equipment like fax machines and computers wears out after time. But when it comes to real estate, most property owners don't live long enough, or keep their buildings long enough, for them to wear out. Therefore, the tax saving from the deduction is a profit that is added to your overall financial return.

There are a few different methods that you can use to determine your annual depreciation allowance. The most common method relies on using the land-to-improvement ratios found on your property tax bill. Don't be concerned if the actual dollar amount shown on the tax bill doesn't mesh with what you're paying for the property; it is the ratio we are looking for. The idea is to use the ratio numbers to get the percentage you need to determine the value of the improvements. To do this, use the following calculation:

Assessed improvement value ÷ Total assessed value
= % Value of improvements

Once you know the percentage value of the improvements, you then multiply that by the sales price to get the amount of depreciable improvements:

% Value of improvements × Price = Depreciable improvements

Keep in mind that you don't have to establish your depreciation schedule until you file your tax return. In most cases, there will usually be sufficient time between the property closing and the tax filing deadline to discuss the method you want to use with your tax professional.

MODIFIED ACCELERATED COST RECOVERY SYSTEM (MACRS)

The tax code change in 1986 established the Modified Accelerated Cost Recovery System (MACRS). This code established the recovery period, or useful life, of assets to be depreciated. Like much of the government's tax code, these periods usually bear no correlation to reality with regard to the useful life of an asset. Nonetheless, in the case of improved property there are two classes of property and two recovery periods that were established. They are:

Type of Property	Recovery Period/Useful Life
Residential	27.5 Years
Nonresidential	39 Years

Note that it doesn't matter what the true age of your property is; if your property is residential, you use 27.5 years. If your property is categorized as nonresidential, you use 39 years. Additionally, when using this method of depreciation, you will have the same amount of annual depreciation expense over the entire useful life of the building. To arrive at the annual expense, you simply divide the value of the depreciable improvements by the recovery period, which gives you your deduction.

Now let's take a look at the calculation using the example property. First we find the value of the improvements and then divide that value by the recovery period. We are paying $279,000 for the property and are using the land and improvement ratios from the tax bill as described earlier. The tax bill shows the improvements assessed at $40,000 and the total assessed value of the property at $65,000. We would then calculate the depreciation allowance as follows:

$$\$40,000 \text{ Improvements} \div \$65,000 \text{ Total assessed}$$
$$\text{value} = 61.5\% \text{ Improvements}$$

We would then multiply the sales price by the improvement percentage to get the amount of depreciable improvements:

$$\$279,000 \times 61.5\% = \$171,585 \text{ Depreciable improvements}$$

Finally, to determine our annual appreciation allowance, we divide the depreciable improvements by the recovery period:

$$\$171,585 \div 27.5 = \$6,239 \text{ Annual depreciation allowance}$$

Before we can determine what kind of savings our depreciation allowance gives us, we first need to review two other code changes made in the tax reform of 1986. They are important because these changes limit your ability to use the excess depreciation to shelter the income from your other job.

The first new code change classifies real estate investors into either "active" or "passive" investors. Passive investors are defined as those who buy property as limited partners or with a group of more than ten other partners. As a passive investor, you can use the depreciation deduction to shelter any profit from the property. Any excess write-off must be carried forward to be used as the profit from the building increases. The theory is that this money is like having a savings account of tax benefits that can be drawn on to cover future profits.

An active investor is one who buys the property alone or with just a couple of partners who are "materially participating" in the management of the building. By materially participating, the IRS means that you have a say in how the building runs. Even if you have hired management to care for day-to-day operations, you materially participate in the property and are an "active investor," according to the IRS, if the buck stops with you.

Additionally, the IRS has categorized investors into two different types:

1. Those who invest in real estate in addition to their regular career

2. Those who consider real estate investing and management as their primary career

Most investors fall into the category in which real estate is something they do in addition to their regular career. If this describes you, then your real estate losses will be limited to $25,000. For example, your adjusted gross income before real estate deductions is $50,000 and your losses from property are $30,000. In this scenario, you would only be able to deduct $25,000 of the $30,000. But don't fret; you don't lose the remaining $5,000. Instead, it would go into that tax-sheltered bank account mentioned earlier. What this deduction means is that instead of paying tax on $50,000 of income, you only pay tax on $25,000. And because the tax you save is a profit, it is therefore included in the overall return from your investment.

From a realistic perspective, assuming your properties run at a break-even cash flow or better, this threshold of $25,000 takes a long time to reach. In fact, with the MACRS depreciation and an improvement ratio of 70 percent, you would have to own almost $1,000,000 worth of property to reach $25,000 of excess depreciation. As your properties become more profitable, you can use more of the depreciation to shelter the property income and have less to shelter your regular career income.

Another code change from the Tax Reform Act of 1986 limits your ability to use the losses from your real estate against the earnings from your regular career. This limit applies when your earnings exceed $100,000, after which you will lose $1 of deduction for every $2 you earn over $100,000. This would mean that at $150,000 you would have no deduction against your income. But remember, these are not lost; they are just saved for future use.

Now, knowing all that, let's go back to our two-unit example and calculate your tax benefit. We will assume you are an active investor in the 28 percent federal tax bracket. To calculate your tax savings, we need to first shelter the taxable profit from the property. As you will recall, you have a taxable cash flow of $12 and a taxable equity growth from loan reduction of $2,668 per year. We calculate the carryover loss as follows:

Depreciation Allowance	$6,239
Less Cash Flow	– $ 12
Less Equity Growth	– $2,668
Tax-sheltered Benefit	$3,559

The tax savings is calculated by multiplying the tax bracket by the sheltered benefit:

Tax-Sheltered Benefit	$3,559
Tax Rate	× 28%
Tax Savings	$ 997

Besides federal taxes, many states require you to pay state income tax. Their rules are usually similar to the federal rules when it comes to deductions and depreciation. If you live in a state with a tax, you will receive an additional savings, and you can use this same formula to estimate those figures.

PUTTING IT ALL TOGETHER

Now let's look at the total annual tax-deferred return combining all four components. You have a cash flow of $12, equity growth from loan reduction of $2,668, equity growth from appreciation of $13,950, and tax savings of $997. The calculation looks like this:

Cash Flow	$ 12
Loan Reduction	$ 2,668
Appreciation	$13,950
Tax Savings	+ $13,997
Total Return	$17,627

Because you only put $8,370 down with your FHA loan to purchase the property, we can compute the total return as follows:

Total return $17,627 ÷ Down payment $8,370
= 210% Return on investment

At this point you probably doubt our sanity because of the astronomical 210 percent return. One of our goals was to show that it was possible to create some real wealth with a down payment that is affordable to most people. Again, the reason we were able to pull off such a feat is because we used leverage to buy the property (3 percent of your money, 97 percent of the bank's money). Note that if you had put 20 percent down, the percentage return would have been less—still significant but less than the 210 percent return demonstrated above.

FIGURE 5.1
PROPERTY ANALYSIS WORKSHEET

Address:

Basic Return

  1. Value of Property   _____

  2. Loans on Property   _____

  3. Equity in Property (Line 2 – Line 3)

  4. Gross Income   _____ Month × 12 =   _____

  5. Expenses   _____ Month × 12 =   _____

  6. Loan Payments   _____ Month × 12 =   _____

  7. Interest (_____ Loan Amount × _____ %) =   _____

  8. Loan Payoff (Line 6 – Line 7) =   _____

  9. Cash Flow (Line 4 – Line 5 – Line 6) =   _____

10. Depreciation Deduction   _____

11. Tax Shelter (Line 10 – Line 9 – Line 8)   _____

12. Tax Savings (Tax Bracket _____ % × Line 11) =   _____

13. Building Profit (Line 8 + Line 9 + Line 12) =   _____

14. Basic Return (Line 13 ÷ Line 3) =   _____

Return on Equity

15. Cash Flow (Line 9)   _____

16. Loan Payoff (Line 8)   _____

17. Tax Savings (Line 12)   _____

18. Appreciation _____ % × Line 1   _____

19. Total Investment Return (Lines 15 + 16 + 17 + 18)   _____

20. Return on Equity (Line 19 ÷ Line 3)   _____

To save some arithmetic, there are many computer-generated systems for calculating this return. Some are proprietary systems written by their firms, and many are just modified spreadsheet systems. If you have access to one of these systems it will save time, but having an automated system is not necessary. The worksheet in Figure 5.1 will help you calculate the return yourself. All you need is a calculator.

YOUR WINNING LOTTO TICKET

"Long-range planning does not deal with future decisions,
but with the future of present decisions."
—PETER DRUCKER, AUTHOR

As you've noticed by now, our approach to real estate investing is pretty conservative. We've based our example property not on helping you get rich but rather on trying to give you insight into how a relatively small real estate purchase now could fund a safe and plentiful life for you later. In fact, securing that kind of trouble-free peace of mind is the primary reason so many Americans play the lottery week after week. In Chapter 6, we'll show you specifically why investing in real estate is akin to winning your own lottery and, second, how to plan ahead so the numbers you choose will come in.

YOUR WINNING NUMBERS

In the real world it's no secret that it takes money to make money. If you don't have any money to invest, it's going to be tough to make a profit. That's probably why the lottery is so popular; it gives anyone with a buck a chance to be a millionaire. We don't have the magic solution for everyone; however, if you can manage to save just enough to get started investing, at least you'll give yourself a fighting chance at retirement.

SHARING THE SECRETS

Albert Einstein was once asked what the most powerful force in the universe was; without hesitation, he answered, "Compound interest." Years before, Ben Franklin called compound interest "the stone that will turn lead into gold." Combine compound interest with leverage and you get the two components that launch real estate investing into a stratosphere all its own.

Whether we know it or not, compound interest is a fairly well-known principle. If you put money in the bank, the bankers refer to the amount of money you will earn in terms of the "yield." Your yield will be higher than the interest rate quoted on your account. This is because the bank assumes you will be leaving the profit (interest) in the bank along with the original amount you invested. The idea is you will earn interest on the interest. In the end, this process raises the amount you earn on your original investment by leaps and bounds.

A math lesson might help. Here is the formula for calculating how much compound interest will increase your return:

$$FV = PV(1 + I)^n$$

Don't panic; this math really isn't as overwhelming as it looks. What's more, most calculators have this formula built in so it's a snap for the average person to work out. Nonetheless, so you can impress your friends and family, the components of the compound interest algorithm translate this way:

- FV = **Future Value** of the investment you make

- PV = **P**resent **V**alue of that investment

- I = Average **I**nterest rate you earn on the investment

- n = The **n**umber of years you keep your money invested

Simply, this formula will give you an estimate of what the money you have today (PV) will be worth in the future (FV). This estimate is based on the percentage you earn (I) over the years (n) you have your money invested.

For example, if you had $10,000 to invest and could earn just 5 percent on it for the next 20 to 25 years, here's how your money would grow because of the effects of compound interest.

$10,000 @ 5% for 20 years = $26,533

$10,000 @ 5% for 25 years = $33,863

Pretty nice, isn't it? But the story gets even better. To see the real advantage to real estate investing we need to add the second wealth-building concept into this equation: leverage. According to Merriam Webster, leverage is defined as "an increased means of accomplishing some purpose." When it comes to investing, our definition is "Making money using someone else's money." You've probably heard this concept loosely referred to as "other people's money" or "OPM" for short.

What's great is that the entire real estate industry is built around encouraging the use of other people's money to fund these types of investments. The biggest proponent of the concept is the federal government via the Federal Housing Administration (FHA) and the Department of Veterans Affairs (VA). The FHA and VA encourage home ownership by offering financing for homebuyers with low or no down payment programs. The purpose is to encourage people to own their own home. These FHA and VA loans are nothing more than loans designed to take advantage of leverage—leverage that is encouraged by your government.

What's amazing is that so many people take advantage of using borrowed money to buy a home but never take advantage of this idea to make any additional real estate investments that could secure their future for good. These same homeowners marvel at how much their home appreciates over the years, but when it comes to long-term planning, this lightbulb always stays dim. So let's get out of the dark.

As you learned in the previous chapter, one of the great advantages of real estate is that it offers several types of return. The cash flow gives you something to spend today, yet the appreciation creates the big-time wealth for your future via the use of leverage. To demonstrate the effect of leverage, let's talk about just this one component of return from real estate: value appreciation.

The value of property increases in most areas of the country because of inflation and demand. Bread, milk, and gas seem to cost more every year and, thankfully for real estate investors, so does the price of housing. We call that value appreciation. Appreciation rates vary all over the country, but regardless of where you live, most areas always seem to have some steady increase in value as the years go on. (Recall the value appreciation that took place in four separate areas of the country in Chapter 4.) To demonstrate how this will work to your benefit we'll use a rate of 5 percent appreciation for the following example. If you own a property worth $100,000, this means that it will go up 5 percent in price every year. If you paid all cash for your house, that means you earn 5 percent on your $100,000, which is $5,000.

Paying all cash for a property, however, isn't what makes real estate investors money. Rather, it's using leverage to its full advantage that creates their real wealth. The idea is to use a little bit of your own money, lots of someone else's, and then reap the rewards of 100 percent of the investment. Here's an illustration of a return after one year of ownership assuming two different down payment options. We'll use a 20 percent down payment (the amount it would take with a conventional loan) and a 3 percent down payment (offered on many properties through FHA) and factor in the same modest 5 percent appreciation rate as before. Here is what is possible:

Down Payment	Appreciation	Percentage Return on Down Payment
$20,000	$5,000	25%
$ 3,000	$5,000	167%

As you can see, a return of 167 percent isn't anything to scoff at. Especially when you compare it to the meager returns you can get on your money at the bank or credit union. Even the 25 percent return from the 20 percent down payment scenario looks great compared to most other investments. And remember, value appreciation is only one component of return from an investment in real estate. This investment, as you know, will help you make money three other ways (cash flow, loan reduction, and tax benefits), and it's the combination of all the returns that creates the kind of money needed to fund a retirement worth smiling about.

For the pièce de résistance, let's work that compound interest formula again by adding leverage (your money + the borrowed money) into the mix. Even though our example showed a 25 percent return from appreciation alone, we will be ultraconservative and scale back to just a 20 percent return.

$10,000 @ 20% for 20 years = $383,367

$10,000 @ 20% for 25 years = $953,962

Yes, you read those numbers right. Amazing isn't it? Though we used the same $10,000 initial investment, our return this time shot through the roof! In fact, so much so that you could fund a pretty great future on those kinds of figures—all due to using compound interest and its best friend, leverage.

Now that you can see how to hit the lottery, let's learn how to put together a plan so you can actually do it for yourself.

COMPONENTS OF YOUR PLAN

Although good investment plans do not start out in minute detail, you should put your ideas down on paper from day one. To get things started, buy yourself a sturdy three-ring binder to put your plan in. This way, you can change the contents easily as you make purchases and progress over the years. Divide your planning binder into the following four sections:

1. Goals

2. General plan

3. Detailed plan

4. Follow-up and goal review

In the remainder of this chapter we will go over each of these sections of your plan in detail.

GOALS

This section of your plan is its lifeblood. Here you will lay out your long-term investment goals and the time frame you have scheduled for their achievement. The goals section of your investment plan should be divided into the following five subsections:

1. Cash-flow requirements

2. Net-worth projections

3. Tax-sheltered benefits required

4. Cash withdrawal from plan

5. Other goals

Let's look at each of these subsections one at a time.

CASH-FLOW REQUIREMENTS. The cash-flow requirements refer to your cash-flow projections during and after completion of the plan. If you make enough money at your day job, you may not need any cash flow from your real estate. If so, that would be great as you'll be able to plow any cash flow you create right back into your buildings. On the other hand, a little bit of extra cash each month might be just what you need. Your retirement fund will suffer a bit, but your day-to-day existence will be all the better for it.

The point at which you will begin to achieve a significant cash flow depends on two things:

1. The initial amount of cash you invest in the plan

2. How well you manage your plan

Cash flow is generated from a property in two ways. The first is by looking at what remains after you pay all the expenses and outstanding loans each month. This cash flow should increase yearly as you increase rents. By the time you retire, this cash flow can be considerable, depending on the amount of financing you have left on your buildings.

The second source of cash flow comes from the eventual sale of the building and carrying your equity as a note against the property. As a general rule, the cash flow at that time will be equal to the going rate of interest multiplied by the net equity of your property. For many retirees, selling their buildings and carrying some (or all) of the paper will give them a much higher return on their nest eggs as compared to the typical savings account, certificate of deposit, or other investment.

Another benefit is that by carrying the financing on a property, you postpone the capital gains taxes due. Uncle Sam says that as long as you're receiving interest only and not getting any principal payments, your capital gains tax will be postponed because the government considers this an installment sale.

YOUR FUTURE NET WORTH. Your net-worth projection is the amount of money you want to be worth at the end of a given period of time. If your lump-sum gap from Chapter 2 showed that you were $500,000 short for retirement, your net-worth projection might look like this:

"Attain a net worth of $500,000 for retirement at the end of a 15-year real estate investment plan."

As we have shown, net worth and cash flow are related. In cases where your investment plan is set up as a retirement vehicle, your net-worth projections will probably be 10 to 12 times your net annual cash-flow requirements. This assumes that at the time of retirement you will be able to locate savings investments that offer yields of from 8 to 10 percent per annum. Based on the available returns for the past 10 to 20 years, this is a pretty reasonable assumption.

You may wish to set your net-worth projections for reasons other than just cash-flow requirements. Remember all the extras we thought up at the end of Chapter 2, things such as cabins, boats, and college tuition for grandchildren? This is where you declare that those things will happen—by factoring the necessary money into your projection. By putting it down on paper today, you'll set the stage for it to come true tomorrow.

TAX BENEFITS. In this section of your planning binder you should write out what kinds of tax benefits you plan to achieve. Tax-sheltered benefits in real estate investments are complicated and can vary widely. Therefore, we have devoted an entire chapter later in this book to this subject. For now, we will provide a few necessary guidelines for you to keep in mind:

- We don't recommend that you buy real estate for tax benefits only. Even though there are lots of great tax advantages to owning investment real estate, many of them have been diluted with the tax law changes in the late 1980s.

- It is important to consider the amount of depreciable improvements when making your final decision on which building to purchase. Remember that the property with the highest land-to-improvement ratio will give you the highest write-off and, thus, the best return.

- If necessary, consider using installment sales to create cash flow during the life of your plan.

- Use 1031 tax-deferred exchanges to grow your nest egg.

Given these guidelines, a reasonable tax goal might be as follows:

"Maximize tax benefits on real estate purchases, and use 1031 tax-deferred exchange and installment sales when available."

CASH WITHDRAWAL. It's important to plan in advance for periods when you may want or need to take cash out of your plan. This will give you the opportunity to make provisions for planned expenditures long before you ever need to come up with the money to pay for them. You could put aside money for your children's education, the trip to Australia you've always wanted to take, buying a sailboat, or building that vacation home on the lot you own in the desert. Building in perks for yourself is one of the most important parts of a successful plan and a great way to stay connected to your plan's ultimate success.

Sometimes you may have enough money in your property accounts to pay for the things you want. If that's the case, then you'll be able to keep the status quo on your buildings and still dip in for some of the things you want. Alternatively, significant cash withdrawals can occur in two ways:

1. By selling your property

2. By refinancing your property

OTHER GOALS. This section covers other things you would like to accomplish with some of the earnings from your real estate investments. These could involve donations to charity or help to family and friends. Examples of these types of goals are:

- Buying a time-share condominium as a wedding present for the kids when they get married.

- Donating 10 percent of the expected proceeds from the sale of the Lawndale duplex to Notre Dame's scholarship fund.

- Purchasing a new theater curtain for the local playhouse.

THE GENERAL PLAN

Your general plan will spell out in one sentence how you will achieve your goals over the period of time set forth in your plan. As we have already seen, setting future net worth at a given interest rate also sets future cash flow. Therefore, we will concentrate most of our discussion of the general plan on achieving a given future net worth.

Here is the template for your general plan:

> "I am going to invest $ _____ for _____ years in real estate investments at a sustained rate of return of _____ % and be worth $ _____ at the end of the plan term."

The first step in developing this general plan is figuring out what you can reasonably expect to earn. We teased you with what is possible earlier and now we will show you the real numbers in earnest. The chart in Figure 6.1 shows various combinations of the compound interest formula. It will quickly give you an idea of the kind of future equities you might expect at various times with differing investment amounts.

Going down the left column (Present Value), locate the amount you originally plan to invest in real estate; let's say it's $10,000. Move over one column to the right to locate the number of years you plan on being invested (n); for this example we'll say it will be 20. The columns to the right of that number are the future values (FV) based on the interest you will be earning (I). Here we are being pretty conservative and projecting an average return of 20 percent for your real estate investments. This gives us a final value at the end of 20 years of $383,376. These numbers don't lie—feel free to do the math and see for yourself how they add up. What's more, go ahead and make copies of this chart and post them above your bed, for these are the numbers that will help you quit your day job for good.

FIGURE 6.1
PRESENT VALUE/FUTURE VALUE CHART

Present Value	Number of Years	Interest = 10%	Interest = 20%	Interest = 30%	Interest = 40%
$10,000	5	$ 16,105	$ 24,883	$ 37,129	$ 53,782
	10	$ 25,937	$ 61,917	$ 137,858	$ 289,255
	15	$ 41,772	$ 154,070	$ 511,859	$ 1,555,681
	20	$ 67,275	$ 383,376	$ 1,900,496	$ 8,366,826
$20,000	5	$ 32,210	$ 49,766	$ 74,259	$ 107,565
	10	$ 51,875	$ 123,835	$ 275,717	$ 578,509
	15	$ 83,545	$ 308,140	$ 1,023,718	$ 3,111,362
	20	$134,550	$ 766,752	$ 3,800,993	$16,733,651
$30,000	5	$ 48,315	$ 74,650	$ 111,388	$ 161,347
	10	$ 77,812	$ 185,752	$ 413,575	$ 867,764
	15	$125,317	$ 462,211	$ 1,535,577	$ 4,667,043
	20	$201,825	$1,150,128	$ 5,701,489	$25,100,477
$40,000	5	$ 64,420	$ 99,533	$ 148,517	$ 215,130
	10	$103,750	$ 247,669	$ 551,434	$ 1,157,019
	15	$167,090	$ 616,281	$ 2,047,436	$ 6,222,724
	20	$269,100	$1,533,504	$ 7,601,986	$33,467,302
$50,000	5	$ 80,526	$ 124,416	$ 185,647	$ 268,912
	10	$129,687	$ 309,587	$ 689,292	$ 1,446,273
	15	$208,862	$ 770,351	$ 2,559,295	$ 7,778,405
	20	$336,375	$1,916,880	$ 9,502,482	$41,834,128
$60,000	5	$ 96,631	$ 149,299	$ 222,776	$ 322,694
	10	$155,625	$ 371,504	$ 827,151	$ 1,735,528
	15	$250,635	$ 924,421	$ 3,071,154	$ 9,334,086
	20	$403,650	$2,300,256	$11,402,978	$50,200,953

Now that you can see how compound interest will be your best friend, let's pull all this work together and set your general plan. There are three steps in the process:

1. Determine how much cash you have available to invest comfortably.

2. Set the achievability of your future net worth.

FIGURE 6.2
TRANSACTIONAL POSITION WORKSHEET–BLANK

Starting Year _____
Transactional Position for Real Estate Retirement Plan

Year of Plan	Market Value	Total Equity	Income	Oper'g Exp's	Total Interest	Amorti-zation	Cash Flow	Appre-ciation	Tax Rebate	Return on Equity (ROE) %	Avg. Return on Equity %
	Actual	*Actual*	*__% × Yearly Increase*	*__% × Yearly Increase*	*Actual*	*Actual*	*Actual*	*__% × Market Value*	*Actual*		
1	_____	_____	_____	_____	_____	_____	_____	_____	_____	_____	_____
2	_____	_____	_____	_____	_____	_____	_____	_____	_____	_____	_____
3	_____	_____	_____	_____	_____	_____	_____	_____	_____	_____	_____
4	_____	_____	_____	_____	_____	_____	_____	_____	_____	_____	_____
5	_____	_____	_____	_____	_____	_____	_____	_____	_____	_____	_____
6	_____	_____	_____	_____	_____	_____	_____	_____	_____	_____	_____
7	_____	_____	_____	_____	_____	_____	_____	_____	_____	_____	_____
8	_____	_____	_____	_____	_____	_____	_____	_____	_____	_____	_____
9	_____	_____	_____	_____	_____	_____	_____	_____	_____	_____	_____
10	_____	_____	_____	_____	_____	_____	_____	_____	_____	_____	_____
11	_____	_____	_____	_____	_____	_____	_____	_____	_____	_____	_____
12	_____	_____	_____	_____	_____	_____	_____	_____	_____	_____	_____
13	_____	_____	_____	_____	_____	_____	_____	_____	_____	_____	_____
14	_____	_____	_____	_____	_____	_____	_____	_____	_____	_____	_____
15	_____	_____	_____	_____	_____	_____	_____	_____	_____	_____	_____
16	_____	_____	_____	_____	_____	_____	_____	_____	_____	_____	_____
17	_____	_____	_____	_____	_____	_____	_____	_____	_____	_____	_____
18	_____	_____	_____	_____	_____	_____	_____	_____	_____	_____	_____
19	_____	_____	_____	_____	_____	_____	_____	_____	_____	_____	_____
20	_____	_____	_____	_____	_____	_____	_____	_____	_____	_____	_____

3. Set the number of years you want for the overall plan.

We'll go through the same exercise as before, but this time it won't be a dress rehearsal. Using this chart, move down the column on the far left (Present Value) to the amount nearest your available capital. Move across this row until you come to a value at least as large as your lump-sum gap or your future net-worth goal. The percentage rate at the top of this column is the minimum rate of return you will have to maintain in order to meet your general plan goal in the time you have allotted to achieve it. Remember, you can combine two lines and add the totals to get a combination that equals your capital investment if it isn't on the chart.

THE DETAILED PLAN

The detailed plan in Figure 6.2 is similar to a profit plan of a business. It establishes the year-by-year goals of the plan and will be the yardstick by which to measure how you are doing along the way. Make copies of the worksheet in Figure 6.2 and insert them in your planning binder. You should be adding data to it for as long as you're building your nest egg through real estate.

The horizontal lines represent the year by using year-by-year estimates of the performance of any property you acquire. The vertical columns are the financial parameters of the plan. The most important columns are the last two columns—the Return on Equity (ROE) and Average Return on Equity (AROE). The numbers that are inserted into these columns are the ones that need to stay above the minimum percentage return required to meet your goals in your desired time frame.

To illustrate how to do this and to make it really simple, we will use the $8,370 it took to buy the example Lawndale duplex as our starting capital. We'll use that property as the beginning invest-

FIGURE 6.3

TRANSACTIONAL POSITION WORKSHEET—2002

Starting Year 2002
Transactional Position for Real Estate Retirement Plan

Year of Plan	Market Value	Total Equity	Income	Oper'g Exp's	Total Interest	Amorti- zation	Cash Flow	Appre- ciation	Tax Rebate	Return on Equity (ROE) %	Avg. Return on Equity %
			3.5%× Yearly Increase	2.5%× Yearly Increase				5%× Market Value			
	Actual	Actual	Actual	Actual	Actual	Actual	Actual	Actual	Actual		
1	279,000	8,370	27,000	5,400	18,948	2,664	12	13,950	1,106	212	212
2	___	___	___	___	___	___	___	___	___	___	___
3	___	___	___	___	___	___	___	___	___	___	___
4	___	___	___	___	___	___	___	___	___	___	___
5	___	___	___	___	___	___	___	___	___	___	___
6	___	___	___	___	___	___	___	___	___	___	___
7	___	___	___	___	___	___	___	___	___	___	___
8	___	___	___	___	___	___	___	___	___	___	___
9	___	___	___	___	___	___	___	___	___	___	___
10	___	___	___	___	___	___	___	___	___	___	___
11	___	___	___	___	___	___	___	___	___	___	___
12	___	___	___	___	___	___	___	___	___	___	___
13	___	___	___	___	___	___	___	___	___	___	___
14	___	___	___	___	___	___	___	___	___	___	___
15	___	___	___	___	___	___	___	___	___	___	___
16	___	___	___	___	___	___	___	___	___	___	___
17	___	___	___	___	___	___	___	___	___	___	___
18	___	___	___	___	___	___	___	___	___	___	___
19	___	___	___	___	___	___	___	___	___	___	___
20	___	___	___	___	___	___	___	___	___	___	___

ment of this example and the general investment plan that we just worked out to set our final net worth goal. Here's the general plan:

"We are going to invest $8,370 for 20 years in real estate investments at a sustained rate of return of 20 percent to be worth $320,886 at the end of the plan term."

Given that goal, the next step in building a true detailed plan is to establish accurate variables to be used to make the estimates for the future calculations of the plan. What you will need are:

- Appreciation rate for your area

- Interest rates for first and second loans

- Loan-to-value ratios

- Income and expense increase rates

- Buy and sell costs

- Gross multipliers for various size properties

You will be able to establish these variables after you have conducted some diligent research. Also, don't discount the help that the agent who sold you your property might be able to give. He or she should have access to the prior history of the market, appreciation rates, and all the other variables needed to help establish a detailed plan. We will start this detailed plan with the specifics of the example property at the end of the first year of ownership.

To recap (see Figure 6.3), remember that in our example our return on investment the first year was:

Cash Flow	$ 12
Equity Growth (loan reduction)	$ 2,664
Equity Growth (appreciation)	$13,950
Tax Benefits	$ 1,106
Total	$17,732

FIGURE 6.4
TRANSACTIONAL POSITION WORKSHEET—THREE YEARS

Starting Year 2002
Transactional Position for Real Estate Retirement Plan

Year of Plan	Market Value	Total Equity	Income	Oper'g Exp's	Total Interest	Amorti- zation	Cash Flow	Appre- ciation	Tax Rebate	Return on Equity (ROE) %	Avg. Return on Equity %
			3.5%× Yearly Increase	2.5%× Yearly Increase				5%× Market Value			
	Actual	Actual	Actual		Actual	Actual	Actual	Value	Actual		
1	279,000	8,370	27,000	5,400	18,948	2,664	12	13,950	1,106	212	212
2	292,950	22,320	27,945	5,535	18,757	2,855	798	14,648	1,110	87	149
3	307,598	369,968	28,923	5,673	18,557	3,055	1,638	15,380	1,060	57	118
4	___	___	___	___	___	___	___	___	___	___	___
5	___	___	___	___	___	___	___	___	___	___	___
6	___	___	___	___	___	___	___	___	___	___	___
7	___	___	___	___	___	___	___	___	___	___	___
8	___	___	___	___	___	___	___	___	___	___	___
9	___	___	___	___	___	___	___	___	___	___	___
10	___	___	___	___	___	___	___	___	___	___	___
11	___	___	___	___	___	___	___	___	___	___	___
12	___	___	___	___	___	___	___	___	___	___	___
13	___	___	___	___	___	___	___	___	___	___	___
14	___	___	___	___	___	___	___	___	___	___	___
15	___	___	___	___	___	___	___	___	___	___	___
16	___	___	___	___	___	___	___	___	___	___	___
17	___	___	___	___	___	___	___	___	___	___	___
18	___	___	___	___	___	___	___	___	___	___	___
19	___	___	___	___	___	___	___	___	___	___	___
20	___	___	___	___	___	___	___	___	___	___	___

To make the estimates for the second and succeeding years of the plan, we have used the assumption of a 3.5 percent yearly income increase and a 2.5 percent yearly increase in expenses. For the other components on the chart we have worked out the actual numbers in longhand. This requires a bit of time and arithmetic but is necessary for you to be accurate.

The next chart in Figure 6.4 takes us through the end of the third year of ownership on the Lawndale duplex.

As they say, "The proof is in the pudding." By penciling out your year-by-year transactional position as demonstrated, the idea is that you will be able to stay on track and retire on schedule.

FOLLOW-UP AND GOAL REVIEW

This is the section of your planning binder that you will revisit on a regular basis. Here you should insert predetermined dates to periodically monitor your progress. Certainly more important than assembling a successful plan on paper will be managing that plan to its successful completion. This section of your plan will force you to review and adjust your thinking at each step along the way.

This review of your plan starts with objectively looking at your personal situation and then examining how changes in your life may affect your investments. As things change personally, you will see that you might need to adjust your long-term goals. For example, an unexpected promotion at work may allow you to buy another building sooner than expected. This could get you to your goal sooner, or raise the amount of your final net worth when it comes time to retire. On the other hand, a job change may take away some of the time you had dedicated to the properties and could slow things down. Furthermore, the market and the economy may be changing for better or worse, which would, no doubt, affect what you buy and sell in the coming year.

We recommend you keep a blank copy of the transactional projection worksheet shown earlier in this chapter. At the times when you do this follow-up and goal review, make it a point to meet with your investment real estate agent and do an estimate of value based on the current market conditions. Compare what really happened in that year with the plan you laid out a year earlier. See how you did. If there are any significant changes, go back and revise your plan and get ready for next year. Ask your agent's opinion on how the market is doing and where it looks like it is going in the next 12 months. Use the new value and the actual performance figures from the year's operation of your property to complete the next line of your transactional position worksheet.

No doubt many changes will occur over the life of a long-term real estate investment plan. Some changes will be positive and some will be negative. The secret is to take full advantage of the positives and take the necessary steps to minimize the negatives. This requires keeping informed at all times about what's really happening with you—and the market.

CHAPTER 7

TAX PLANNING

Late one night, just blocks from the Capitol, a mugger jumped into the path of a well-dressed fellow and stuck a gun in his ribs. "Give me your money," the thief demanded. Are you kidding?" the man said, "I'm a U.S. congressman." "In that case," the mugger growled, cocking his weapon, "give me my money."
—PLAYBOY MAGAZINE

Owning investment real estate comes with a slew of tax ramifications. Thankfully, if tax rules are used to their full advantage, the IRS seems to line up clearly on the right side of the investor. Even so, lawmakers often manipulate tax codes to either stimulate or restrain the economy as they see fit. Whether it's making changes to the depreciation schedules or battling back and forth about capital gains laws, the one constant from the IRS is that nothing ever stays the same. Regardless, the tax benefits from owning investment real estate can be substantial. In this chapter we'll explain how Uncle Sam is there to help you retire in style.

There are two broad areas where knowledge of taxation rules are important. The first is during the ownership and management of real estate. The second is on the sale of real estate. Hopefully, both of these areas are ones that you will become intimately familiar with. We'll begin by talking about the tax laws related to ownership and management of real property.

DEDUCTIONS AS AN OWNER

As a property owner, you are allowed, by the IRS, to deduct most of the purchase costs and operating expenses associated with a real estate purchase. The rule says that purchase costs are deductible in the year in which you acquire the property. The following list covers some of the most common items that are deductible:

- Prepaid interest on your loans

- Fire insurance

- Liability insurance

- Property tax prorations

- Escrow fees

- Title insurance costs

- Miscellaneous fees from lender

- Miscellaneous fees from escrow company

Additionally, loan fees and points paid to secure a new loan on income property are also deductible. The difference is that these fees must be paid off over the life of the loan as opposed to in the year of acquisition. For instance, if the loan for our two-unit example property required a loan fee of 1.5 percent and the loan was a 30-year loan, the yearly deduction would first be calculated by multiplying the loan amount by the loan fee rate:

Loan Amount	$270,630
Loan Fee Rate	× .015
Fee (points)	$ 4,059

Then, to determine your yearly deduction, divide the loan fee by the term of the loan:

Loan fee ($4,059) ÷ Term of loan (30 years) = $135.30

As demonstrated, $135.30 would be the yearly deduction. In past years, points could be written off in their entirety in the year of purchase. But after years of abuse, this rule was changed.

OPERATING EXPENSES

Operating expenses for your rental property are deductible in the year you spend the money. The problem is distinguishing between items to be expensed and items to be capitalized. As mentioned, the IRS says that expense items are deductible in the year you spend the money. Capital expenses, however, are a different story. These items must be written off over the period of time they contribute to their useful life under the tax codes.

For those just starting out in this game, distinguishing between capital items and items to be expensed can be tricky. As a general rule, if any improvement you make increases the value or completely replaces a component of the property, it should be considered a capital expenditure and as a result needs to be depreciated over time. In contrast, if the improvement merely maintains the value or corrects a problem at your building, then it should be considered an expense item. Some examples of items you can expense yearly are:

- Utility payments

- Interest on loans

- Taxes

- Insurance premiums

- Gardening and cleaning costs

- Business licenses and city fees

- Plumbing repairs

- Roofing repairs

- Electrical repairs

- Miscellaneous maintenance and repairs

- Property management fees

- Advertising and rental commissions

- Mileage, postage, and phone expenses associated with the operation of the property

- Any other noncapital expenses

As you can see, these items maintained the value and/or corrected problems. Thus, we were able to expense them.

CAPITAL EXPENSES

A capital expense, on the other hand, is money spent on major improvements to rental property, such as building additions and all permanent fixtures on a property. Some examples of capital expenses are:

- Drapes or window coverings

- Carpeting

- New roof

- New plumbing

- New electrical system

- Building additions

- Major appliances or furnishings

- Major repairs—new driveway, replace siding or stucco, replace landscaping, etc.

It is important to note that unlike interest (an item you can expense yearly), the money that goes toward principal each month on your loan payment is not a deductible capital expense. It is actually one of those returns on your investment that you must pay tax on, but don't get the money for. The reason that the part of the payment that goes toward principal reduction is taxable is because it's a profit that comes from tenant income.

THE DEPRECIATION ALLOWANCE

We briefly covered some of the depreciation rules in an earlier chapter, but because these rules are so vital to your bottom-line return, we'll dig a bit deeper.

As the owner of residential income property you are now able to make a deduction for the loss of value to the structure that sits on your property. This deduction is designed to compensate you for the wear and tear that happens to the physical structure of your building from aging. This is not an allowance to cover you for the aging of the land, because land does not wear out or depreciate, yet structures that sit on land do.

The most important component of the depreciation schedule is the land-to-improvement ratio. For any improved property, part of a property's value comes from the dirt, and part of its value comes from the improvements. Because dirt doesn't depreciate, a property that has a high ratio of improvements has a high depreciation deduction.

When determining your depreciation you must remember that you can't just pick your ratio out of thin air. Instead, you must use a method accepted by the IRS. If you don't, the result could be costly. In a worst-case scenario the IRS could audit you, disallow your schedule, and require you to set a new one. Odds are it would end up charging you for additional taxes, penalties, and interest.

The safest method in setting your land-to-improvement ratio is to use the one that the county tax assessor sets on your tax bill. The good news is that the IRS will rarely challenge this ratio, as it would be challenging another government entity. Unfortunately, the ratio determined by the county tax assessor isn't always as accurate as it could be. Alternatively, you could derive your ratio from the appraisal that was conducted when you purchased the property. Using an appraisal is a good idea, especially if the tax assessor's ratio doesn't agree with the actual market.

Once you have established an accurate value of the improvements, the calculation to determine your depreciation deduction that you learned in Chapter 5 is fairly easy.

As a final point, you must remember that the depreciation schedule you originally calculate will be with you as long as you own that property. If you sell the property and pay the taxes due, you can start fresh with a new depreciation schedule on your next building. If you trade up via a 1031 exchange, however, that basis and its schedule stay with you.

CAPITAL GAINS

Capital gains taxes are taxes on the profits you make when you sell your property. To help determine capital gain, you must first learn some new tax terms:

- Sale price: the price you sell your property for

- Adjusted sale price: the net price after subtracting costs of the sale

- Cost basis: the original purchase price plus capital expenses

- Adjusted cost basis: the cost basis less depreciation

Now that you're up to speed on the terminology, capital gains can be estimated by first subtracting the sale costs from the sale price. This computation gives you the adjusted sale price:

$$\begin{array}{r} \text{Sale price} \\ - \underline{\text{Sale costs}} \\ \text{Adjusted sale price} \end{array}$$

To determine the adjusted cost basis, take the cost basis, add in capital expenses, and then subtract depreciation:

$$\begin{array}{r} \text{Cost basis} \\ + \text{Capital expenses} \\ - \underline{\text{Depreciation}} \\ \text{Adjusted cost basis} \end{array}$$

Finally, to determine your capital gain, subtract the adjusted cost basis from the adjusted sale price:

$$\begin{array}{r} \text{Adjusted sale price} \\ - \underline{\text{Adjusted cost basis}} \\ \text{Capital gain} \end{array}$$

Now let's use an illustration with our example property to calculate the capital gain. Remember, we bought the property for $279,000. We've depreciated it for five years at $7,102 per year, which is a total depreciation of $35,510 ($7,102 × 5 = $35,510). Additionally, we just put on a new roof that cost $5,000 (a capital expense). Five years later, we can sell the property for $370,000. Our total expense to sell will be $20,000. Knowing all this, we can calculate our capital gain on a sale by going through the simple calculations you just learned:

Sale Price	$370,000
Less Sale Costs	– 20,000
Adjusted Sale Price	$350,000
Cost Basis	$279,000
Plus Capital Expenses	+ 5,000
Less Depreciation	– 35,510
Adjusted Cost Basis	$248,490
Adjusted Sale Price	$350,000
Adjusted Cost Basis	–248,490
Capital Gain	$101,510

As you see, the capital gain in this scenario would be $101,510. Thankfully, a number of options are available to the real estate investor to help defer paying these taxes. What follows are the methods that help distinguish real estate investing from all other investment vehicles.

THE 1031 TAX-DEFERRED EXCHANGE

When it comes to deferring capital gains taxes, the IRS 1031 tax-deferred exchange is probably the real estate investor's single most important technique available. By using the 1031 exchange, you can pyramid your equity and continue to defer your taxes for years into the future. In effect, the IRS becomes your business partner by letting you use the taxes you owe on your capital gains as a down payment on the buildings you trade into. The government figures that when you trade into larger properties, you will, in turn, make more profit. By making more profit, you will eventually owe more tax. As far as the IRS is concerned, everyone wins. Who said Uncle Sam can't be your friend.

Three rules must be adhered to when qualifying for a 1031 exchange:

1. You must trade for like-kind property. In this instance, like-kind would mean the property you are trading into would be for investment purposes. For example, you can't trade an income-producing duplex for a getaway beach cottage. In contrast, you could trade that duplex for a strip mall or another apartment building. The idea is to trade income-producing property for other income-producing property.

2. The new property should be of equal or greater value than the existing property. This means that you can't trade a duplex that you sold for $300,000 for a triplex worth $290,000. Rather, the new property needs to be worth more than the old one, hence the phrase "trading up."

3. You should not receive cash, mortgage relief, or boot (boot is defined by the IRS as taxable proceeds from a sale other than cash) of any kind in the transaction.

TYPES OF 1031 EXCHANGES

Most 1031 tax-deferred exchanges fall into one of three categories:

1. The straight exchange

2. The three-party exchange

3. The delayed exchange

The straight exchange happens when two parties simply trade properties. At the end of the transaction, each party goes his or her own way. In truth, this scenario doesn't occur that often. Most property owners either trade up or get out all together. By trading straight across the board, one party probably ends up with a lesser property, which fails to meet the requirements of trading into a property of equal or greater value. If this were the case, the party that got the lesser property would have to pay the taxes due, if any.

The second type of exchange, and the most common, is the three-party exchange. As its name suggests, three different parties are involved in the process. One of the key elements of a 1031 exchange is that the party trading up never receives the equity in the property being traded. For that reason, the party cannot just sell the property, collect the proceeds, and go out and buy a larger property. Because most people with bigger properties don't want to trade into anything smaller (and thereby have to pay any tax owed), these three-party exchanges have evolved so that each party can get what it wants and stay within the framework of the law. Here's how a three-party exchange might work:

Facts:

- Andrew owns a triplex and wants to trade into a six-unit building.

- Barry owns a six-unit building and wants to sell, pay his capital gains taxes, and retire along the Gulf of Mexico.

- Charlie is just getting started investing and wants to buy the triplex that Andrew owns.

Solution:

Andrew and Barry enter into an exchange escrow in which Andrew gets the six-unit and Barry gets title to the triplex. In a separate escrow, Barry agrees to accommodate the exchange and deed the triplex to Charlie immediately after he acquires title from Andrew. Both of these escrows contain contingencies stating that they must close concurrently. This means that if Charlie can't buy the triplex for some reason, Barry will not have to take Andrew's triplex in trade for his six-unit.

Result:

At the close, Charlie got started investing and now owns the triplex he wanted, Andrew traded up into the six-unit building he desired, and Barry is relaxing just as planned: in retirement, sipping drinks with little umbrellas in them along the Gulf of Mexico.

In case you were wondering, Barry doesn't pay any tax by taking the title to the triplex because it is sold for the same price at which it was taken in trade. This is what is called a nontaxable event.

The last type of exchange is the delayed or "Starker" exchange. Starker refers to one of the principals in *T.J. Starker v. United States,* a case from the U.S. Court of Appeals for the Ninth Circuit. In this case, Starker swapped some timber acreage for 11 different parcels of property owned by the Crown Zellerbach Corporation. As agreed between the parties, Starker chose the properties, and they were conveyed to him by way of the exchange. It was deemed a delayed exchange because the process spanned more than two years.

Because of the two-year delay, Uncle Sam questioned whether it was an exchange at all and took Starker to federal court. Fortunately for all of us, the court of appeals approved of the process, which has since been codified nationally for use by all U.S. real estate investors. The *Starker* court held that:

1. A simultaneous transfer of title was not required.

2. Internal Revenue Code (IRC) section 1031 should be broadly interpreted and applied. Treasury regulations under IRC section 1001 to the contrary were held invalid.

Once the *Starker* court made its rulings, a number of additional changes were made to IRC 1031. These changes included:

1. Partnership interests are no longer like-kind for exchange purposes.

2. The exchange property the taxpayer desires to receive must be identified within 45 days after the date on which the taxpayer transfers his or her property in the exchange.

3. The taxpayer must receive the identified property within the earlier of 180 days after the date he or she transfers his or her property in the exchange, or the due date of his or her tax return for the year of the exchange, including extensions.

To accomplish a delayed exchange, an accommodator is used. An accommodator is an unrelated party or entity that holds the exchange proceeds and then purchases the trade properties to complete the exchange. In choosing an accommodator you need to exercise due care. Remember that all the funds from your sale will be in its hands until you close on your up-leg property. To that end, make sure you check out your accommodator's credentials through the better business bureau and your state real estate department.

One final issue that exchanges create is related to the goals from your investment plan. While the use of the exchange allows you to pyramid equities, it also pyramids the tax liability on a future sale. If you had plans of cashing out and paying your taxes before retiring, this could leave you with a big tax bill. Instead, you might consider one of two other options. Either pay your taxes as you go along or consider the next alternative, the installment sale.

THE INSTALLMENT SALE

The installment sale is another significant technique for deferring payment of capital gains taxes. Here, sellers elect not only to sell property but also to put up some or all of the financing needed to make the deal work. Because the property is being sold now but paid for later, such deals are called "installment sales." Where taxes are concerned, an installment sale differs from the 1031 exchange because you actually sell the property without getting a new one in return, but you still defer paying some or most of your capital gains taxes. Here's how:

Until you actually receive the profit from the sale of your property, you don't owe the IRS a penny. Instead, with an installment sale you would be carrying the note (and your profit from the sale) long term and receiving interest-only payments from the buyer. The idea is to keep earning a high interest on the taxes due for many years. By doing this you would delay paying the capital gains until the contract is complete.

The rules for qualifying for an installment sale were significantly modified by the Installment Sales Revision Act of 1980. In the past there were rules regarding the amount of down payment and the number of years needed to qualify. These no longer exist. The advantage of an installment sale now is that you are required to pay capital gains tax only on the amount of the profit you receive in one year. You pay the balance of the tax due as you collect the profit in subsequent years.

Because an installment sale can be relatively complex, we will simplify our example. Let's assume you are selling the Lawndale duplex outright and need to decide how to handle the tax on the

$101,150 capital gain we calculated earlier. We'll estimate the tax rate at 28 percent. To find your after-tax net equity, use the following formula:

Capital Gain	$101,510
Tax Rate	× .28
Tax Due	$ 28,423

Once you know the tax due, subtract it from your capital gain to determine your net:

Capital Gain	$101,510
Less Tax	− 28,423
Remaining Profit	$ 73,087

This $73,087 is all your money to do with as you see fit. If you had no plans to spend the money but rather plan to invest it in some passive cash-flow generating vehicle to help with retirement, then the installment sale is for you. As mentioned, with an installment sale, instead of selling the property, getting all cash and walking, you become one of the lenders on the property. You find a qualified buyer and instead of getting new financing, the buyer takes over your existing loan and you carry a loan for the balance of your equity. The only tax due will be on the amount of cash you take as a down payment.

Let's assume you sell the example property for $370,000 and are willing to take a 10 percent down payment and carry the balance of the paper on an installment contract. Here is how this scenario could affect the net:

Down Payment (10%)	$37,000
Tax Rate	× .28
Tax Due	$10,360

To determine the net cash profit, subtract the tax due from the down payment:

Down Payment	$37,000
Less Tax	-$10,360
Net Cash Profit	$26,640

Finally, to determine the balance of the equity from the installment note, subtract the down payment from the capital gain:

Capital Gain	$101,510
Less Down Payment	-$ 37,000
Installment Note	$ 64,510

In this example, we have a net cash profit of $26,640 and an installment note on the property of $64,510.

In the following illustrations you will see how the real advantage of an installment sale comes from what you earn from the installment note, as opposed to putting your net cash in the bank. Let's assume you can get 6 percent interest on your savings from a certificate of deposit or a similar investment. Because you can often earn greater yields by carrying the paper on loans, we'll assume that you can carry this financing at 9 percent interest.

For starters, let's illustrate what the profit on a CD or on a similar investment would look like:

Cash-Out Profit	$73,087
Interest Rate	× .06
Profit	$ 4,385
Monthly Return	$ 365

As you can see, $4,385 divided by 12 months gives you a monthly return of $365. In contrast, here is the return on an installment note:

Installment Note	$64,510
Interest Rate	× .09
Profit	$ 5,806
Monthly Return	$ 484

Even though the installment note was for less money than the cash-out money you put in the bank, your monthly yield was higher because you were able to charge the buyer a higher interest rate on the 90 percent that you financed. As for the 10 percent down payment, here is what that would do for you at 6 percent in the bank:

Net Down Payment	$26,640
Interest Rate	× .06
Profit	$ 1,598
Monthly Return	$ 133

Finally, by adding the profit from the installment note and the 10 percent cash down payment that you put in the bank, you would get the following:

Installment Profit	$5,806
10% Down @ 6% Interest	+$1,598
Installment Total	$7,407
Per Month	$ 617

As you can see, if you divide the total installment profit by 12 months, you create an income for yourself of $617 per month. Obviously, the difference between $617 per month versus $365 per month is quite dramatic. There are two main reasons for the difference:

1. You can usually get a significantly higher interest return on your money by carrying financing versus putting it in a bank or in a comparable investment.

2. You are earning interest on the capital gains you have yet to pay the IRS.

Varying the amount of down payment you accept can increase this interest profit even more. In theory, because you are the banker on your loan, you could agree to a zero down deal and only require interest-only payments. By doing so you would not have to pay any tax whatsoever at this time. Instead, you could be earning 9 percent on your entire note instead of the net after taxes being invested at 6 percent.

REFINANCING

There is one more technique to avoid paying the taxes due on some of the profit from your real estate. This is by securing new financing to pay off the existing loan and net additional cash at the closing because of the increased value of the property. If you are still in the equity-building years of our plan, you will probably use that money to acquire an additional property. One of the great advantages of getting at some of the profit using this method is that there is no tax due on the money. Because we "borrowed" the money from the bank, we have to pay it back, and therefore, not only do we not have to pay any tax, but right now we can write off the interest as a deduction on the property.

Owners who have properties that are managed particularly well prefer this technique. What's more, if you've managed your property correctly, the increased rents should more than cover any increased mortgage payments. If you are in a market where you can pull out most of your equity to move into another property and still keep the original property, you could be well on your way to creating a comfortable retirement scenario for yourself.

To sum up a long and complicated chapter, this information is designed to give you a basic understanding of real estate taxation and some tax-deferral methods. The goal is to make you aware of the complexity of this area so you will seek the advice of your tax expert before you make any move. When it comes to taxes, even minor mistakes could be costly. To that end, we recommend the following.

First, before you ever list a property for sale, make sure you schedule a general review meeting with your tax consultant. Review your goals, discuss all the alternatives, and get a general idea of your position. Second, when listing a property for sale make clear to your agent and in the listing contract that any transaction must be reviewed and approved by your tax consultant. And, finally, when negotiating a potential sale or exchange, include a contingency that gives you a right to have the final purchase agreement reviewed and approved by your tax consultant. This will give you an out if your tax expert advises you against the transaction.

CHAPTER 8

APPRAISING VALUE

"A pint of sweat saves a gallon of blood."
—GEORGE S. PATTON, JR., GENERAL

For those just getting their feet wet in real estate investing, picking that first property can be a knee-knocking experience. Of course, the objective is to make your choice based on purely economic parameters. But clearly, when it comes to taking a risk with your own hard-earned money, that can be easier said than done. Many times, when it comes to deciding between Property "A" and Property "B," emotions will take over and attempt to dictate what you should buy. Many novice investors indignantly declare, "I refuse to purchase any building that I wouldn't live in." If you recognize yourself making that statement, you should realize that you're on the verge of leaving lots of great opportunities behind for someone else to discover.

But don't fret, you are not alone. In fact, it's easy to see why emotions rule the day—you're fearful of losing what little money you have been able to save. In fact, many will argue that the fear of losing their nest egg is as much (if not more of) a motivator as is the promise of gain from investing it. To illustrate, let's say you were invited to a get-together at 9 PM to learn about a business opportunity that could very well make you $1,000 on a $5,000 investment. After a bit of thought, you might decide to spend that time watching the news or *Seinfeld* reruns on TV instead. But let's turn the tables: What would happen if you got a call and were told you would lose that $1,000 if you didn't go to the 9 PM meeting? Precisely.

There is no shame in a bit of apprehension. In fact, playing the devil's advocate will usually help you make prudent decisions along the way. But beware unfounded fear about losing money by buying the "wrong" building could very well keep you from obtaining just the perfect fit for your long-term plan. Thankfully, unlike investing in commodities such as stocks and bonds via the advice of a so-called expert, there are concrete things you can do in this game that will minimize the risk of ever overpaying for a building, namely, learning how to value property accurately for yourself. Expert help is nice, but when it comes to protecting your own nest egg, the peace of mind that will come from conducting your own analysis will be nothing short of invaluable.

This chapter continues your education with a lesson on appraising value. We will teach you the same three classic methods of valuing property used by professional real estate appraisers. From here on, you should be able to buy real estate without the fear of ever losing your shirt.

METHODS OF VALUING PROPERTY

Establishing the value of a piece of real estate can be a tricky job. Fortunately, there are a number of accepted methods of establishing value estimates. We will review each of these appraisal techniques and show you how to use them. The three commonly accepted appraisal methods used by professional appraisers are:

1. Comparative market analysis

2. Reproduction cost

3. Capitalization of income

COMPARATIVE MARKET ANALYSIS

"Comparative market analysis" means nothing more than doing some comparison shopping before you buy any real estate. Just as you would compare and shop prices before buying new furniture or a car, so, too, you need to compare and shop prices for similarly situated properties before making a purchase. The difference in this instance is that you are comparing a building that is for sale with ones that have already been sold.

What do you need to compare? The major considerations are:

- Number of units

- Square footage of the improvements (structure)

- Square footage of the lot (the dirt)

- Condition of the surrounding neighborhood

- Age and condition of the building

- Income-producing capability (current rents versus market rents)

- Parking (garages, pads, carports, or none)

- Amenities (view, fireplaces, multiple baths, pool, patios or decks, etc.)

The idea when conducting a comparative market analysis is to locate a few properties in the same or similar neighborhood that have recently been sold. As outlined previously, look for properties that have traits similar to the one you want to buy. In a perfect world, the sales should be within the past six months—the more recent, the better. Once you gather all the data, your job is to compare and contrast it to determine a fair price for the building you're considering. Here's an illustration.

Let's say that you want to buy the example property we mentioned earlier. Remember, this property consists of two houses on one 5,197-square-foot lot, which were built in 1948. The mix has two one-bedroom houses that are in good condition. The owner wants $279,000 for this property. Is that a fair price? We'll see.

After checking with a few local brokers and appraisers, let's further assume that you are able to locate three comparative sales (comps). We'll call these comps Properties "X," "Y," and "Z." Here's what we know about those properties.

Property "X" also has two houses and looks like it may have been built by the same contractor as the property you want to buy. The difference is both units have two bedrooms each (the Lawndale duplex has one one-bedroom and one two-bedroom). Property "X" also has nicer landscaping. This property sold two months ago for $293,900.

Property "Y" is an attached duplex, was also built in 1948, and is the same size and condition as your property. The units have open parking instead of garages. This building sold a few months ago for $264,000.

Finally, Property "Z" is also just like the property you want except that it sold one year ago for $262,000. Because the sale occurred so long ago, it may be less relevant, albeit still important, to analyze, for there aren't any other comps available.

Here's a recap:

	Proposed Property	Property "X"	Property "Y"	Property "Z"
Price	$279,000	$293,900	$264,000	$262,000
Footage	same	+40 sq. ft.	same	same
Condition	same	same	same	same
Location	same	same	same	same
Lot size	5,197	50 × 100	50 × 100	50 × 100
Garages	2	2	none	4
Sale date	unsold	3 months ago	2 months ago	12 months ago

Because there are differences between the properties, some adjustments must be made. For example, Property "X" has four total bedrooms instead of three, so an adjustment will have to be made in the price of Property "X." To do so, the value of the extra bedroom must be estimated. A little research determined that the cost of building in this area is $85 a square foot. The extra bedroom has 140 square feet. Therefore, this extra room added an additional $11,900 to the price (140 × $85 = $11,900).

Similarly, Property "Y" also must be adjusted because it lacks any garage. For purposes of this analysis, we have determined the cost of building a garage in this area is $30 per square foot. Therefore, the cost of adding 300 square feet to build the missing garages would be $9,000 ($30 × 300 = $9,000).

The adjustment to Property "Z" is more difficult because so much time has gone by since it was sold. The key thing to understand here is the degree to which property in this area has appreciated in the past year. Let's assume that the appreciation rate over the past year is 5 percent. This means that Property "Z" would have increased $13,100 over the past year ($262,000 × 5% = $13,100). So we would need to add that amount to the sale price of Property "Z."

Here's a recap of the adjustments:

	Proposed Property	Property "X"	Property "Y"	Property "Z"
Price	$279,000	$293,900	$264,000	$262,000
Adjust	0	– $11,900	+ $9,000	+ $13,100
Value	$279,000	$282,000	$273,000	$275,100

By adding the three determined values together and then dividing by three we get an average price of $276,667. Thus, as we can see, an asking price of $279,000 for our proposed property seems just about right using this method of analysis.

REPRODUCTION COST APPROACH

Another way to estimate the actual value of a property is to use what is known as the "reproduction cost method." That is, what would it cost to build that same building today? Here you pretend to buy a lot at today's value and then build a "used" building that matches the existing building. For this reason alone, this is not an easy method. It requires a good knowledge of the market for raw land as well as an understanding of the costs of construction and depreciation. Consequently, this method is often used solely by professional real estate appraisers.

If you want to attempt it, the first thing to consider is the cost of the lot. Contact brokers and builders in your area. Find out what similar lots cost. In our example, the lots are about 5,200 square feet. After some diligent research on your part, let's say that in your area, land that size is worth $135,000.

Step two is to figure out what it would cost to build your building. Analyze the square footage and construction method of the property you want to buy. Let's say that the cost to build a standard wood-frame and stucco building like the one you want to buy is $85 per square foot, and the cost to build the garages is $30 per square foot. Given those parameters, the following chart shows the total cost to build a new building in today's market:

	Square Feet	Cost	Total
Building	1,658	$85	$140,930
Garages	300	30	$ 9,000
Amenities	N/A	N/A	$ 20,000
Total			$169,930

So far we have determined that $169,930 is the cost to build a brand-new building. But remember the rub: the Lawndale duplex that we are considering is not new, rather it's 55 years old. The tricky part then is determining the depreciation of this building. Unfortunately, this kind of advanced math usually requires expert knowledge on the part of a professional appraiser. Therefore, for this example we will make an estimate of $20,000 as the amount to depreciate; hence, an actual value for the building is $149,930 ($169,930 – $20,000 = $149,930). Here's how the numbers add up:

Cost of Lot	$135,000
Depreciated Value of Buildings	$149,930
Total	$284,930

As you can see, using the reproduction cost method, we can estimate the value of the Lawndale duplex to be $284,930.

CAPITALIZATION OF INCOME

The last method of appraising real estate value is called the "capitalization of income" approach. This method determines a building's value based on its profitability. In the real world of appraising, different methods of valuing property are used for different types of buildings. With single-family homes, the comparative method is used most often. The reproduction cost method is usually employed for specialized properties (like a church) and for new construction. But for investment property of multiple units, the capitalization of income method is best.

This is probably the most difficult of the three methods to use properly when valuing income property, but actually it is the preferred method. Here's how it works:

For starters, it might help to think of capitalization rates as interest rates. When you put money in the bank you ask, "What interest rate will I get?" Capitalization rates are the same thing. Let's assume you have $10,000 in a savings account, and at the end of the year you earned $500 in interest. The following formula will show your interest rate:

$$\text{Interest earned} \div \text{Amount invested} = \text{Interest rate}$$

Or plugging the savings account numbers into the equation, we get:

$$\$500 \div \$10,000 = 5\%$$

Similarly, to determine the capitalization rate on a building, divide the net income by its price. Net income is determined by subtracting the operating expenses from the gross income. The equation looks like this:

$$\text{Gross income} - \text{Operating expenses} \div \text{Price} = \text{Capitalization rate}$$

Or

$$\text{Net income} \div \text{Price} = \text{Capitalization rate}$$

Using this formula you can calculate the capitalization rate (or interest rate) you will earn on any investment you are considering. Once you know the capitalization rate of your proposed property, you then can determine its value. To do so, you need to change the formulas as follows:

Gross income – Operating expenses ÷ Capitalization rate = Price

Simplified, this becomes

Net income ÷ Capitalization rate = Price

Because this valuation method is so useful, it behooves you to really understand how to use it. To do so accurately, you need to know a few things about the proposed property, including:

- The gross income

- The operating expenses

- The capitalization rate investors expect in the area where the property is located

Let's review each one.

THE GROSS SCHEDULED INCOME. Gross income is the total amount of money the property will bring in in a year, including rent, laundry income, garage rentals, vending sales, and anything else. This is often referred to as the "gross scheduled income" or GSI.

Although determining the GSI should be a pretty straightforward matter, one issue sometimes arises when the current owner has underrented some or all of the units. This is a surprisingly common issue with smaller units, for many passive investors get happy with a certain, reliable level of profit and don't want to risk rocking the boat by attempting to raise rents.

How is this issue handled? Typically, appraisers will make an allowance for market rents, while bankers don't; and investors look for underrented properties, for they can mean lower sales prices but potentially higher profits down the road.

EXPENSES. What does it cost to run this property? That is the next component to understand. Expenses include such things as:

- Property taxes

- Insurance premiums

- Utilities

- Gardening costs

- Management fees

- Maintenance and repair costs

- Vacancies, etc.

Note that you will not be including interest expense here for the capitalization-of-income approach assumes you paid all cash for your building (even though you didn't).

Although getting an accurate analysis of expenses may be easier said than done, it is still imperative that you do so. One owner might not pay for professional management yet another may, and one owner may have rents too low and another may be right on. Whatever the case, finding out what the expenses actually are is critical to determining if the property is a sound investment.

Often, appraisers are forced to estimate the expenses for a certain property based on the type of property that is being appraised and the area where it is located. Obviously, a duplex with no amenities has far less expenses than a full-security building with tennis courts and extensive landscaping does. Similarly, the cost of heating a building in Boston, for example, will be considerably more than heating one in Arizona. Remember that these types of size and regional differences must be accounted for when analyzing expenses.

To equalize these differences, appraisers often use tables of expenses based on a percentage of the gross income. Similarly, if you're conducting an analysis and need to estimate expenses, you too can use the following guidelines as a starting point:

Number of Units	Expense Estimate
2-4	25% of Income
5-15	25% - 35% of Income
15 and up	30% - 45% of Income

Note that these guidelines are the ones we use in the Southern California market. Make sure you seek out the advice of experts in your area, as there are many area-sensitive variables that could be important to factor in, which may change the percentage expense estimates you use.

THE CAP RATE. The final item needed for this valuation method is the expected capitalization rate. The capitalization rate is determined by understanding how much of a return investors can expect to realize in a particular market. The rate will vary in different parts of the country, in different parts of a city, even in buildings within a few blocks of each other.

Additionally, residential, commercial, and industrial properties also have varying capitalization rates. Remember, because the capitalization rate measures the profitability of an investment, certain types of properties involve other risks and thus dissimilar profit possibilities.

Let's see how this method of appraisal is used. For example, the total rental income for the Lawndale duplex in our example is $27,000 and expenses are 20 percent of the gross income, which comes to $5,400 for the year. After speaking with various local appraisers, you conclude that the capitalization rate is 7.5 percent.

Putting this all together, you can calculate the value of the property as follows:

Gross Annual Income	$27,000
Less Operating Expenses	– $ 5,400
Net income	$21,600

Recall that the formula to find value is:

Net income ÷ Capitalization rate = Price

Thus:

$21,600 (Net income) ÷ .075 (Capitalization rate) = $288,000

Using this method, you can see that the value of the property is estimated at $288,000.

TO SUM UP

Now that we've determined value using all three classic methods of appraisal, let's recap the values and come up with an average for all three.

Comparative Analysis Value	$276,667
Reproduction Cost Value	$284,930
Capitalization Value	$288,000
Averaged Value	$283,199

As you can see, by averaging the three methods we came up with a value of $283,199. With a list price of just $279,000 for this property, we have determined that we could even pay full price for this property and still feel like we made a smart purchase.

THE GROSS RENT MULTIPLIER

Sometimes you need a quick way to analyze the value of a building—a way that can get you to the bottom line fast. When this is the case, it is good to know about a method called "the gross rent multiplier." Similar to a price-earnings ratio when valuing a stock, the gross rent multiplier presupposes there is a number—the gross rent multiplier—that you can multiply by the gross income of a property to quickly estimate its value.

Here's how you determine that magic number, the gross rent multiplier:

Price of property ÷ Gross income = Gross rent multiplier

For our example property in Lawndale, the calculation would be:

$279,000 (Price) ÷ $27,000 (Gross income)
= 10.33 (Gross rent multiplier)

So 10.33 is the gross rent multiplier. Once you know that, it's pretty easy to determine the value of your proposed property. Multiply the gross income of the property by the gross rent multiplier:

Gross income × Gross rent multiplier = Value of the property

The following chart will show the effect of several gross rent multipliers on the value of our example:

Gross Income		Gross Rent Multiplier	Value of Property
$27,000	×	9.5	$256,500
$27,000	×	10.0	$270,000
$27,000	×	10.5	$283,500

As you can see, a little difference in the gross rent multiplier can make a big difference in the perceived value of a property. The thing to understand about using the gross rent multiplier method is that it is simply that—a gross calculation—and simple things can throw your analysis off, such as:

1. If a property owner has kept the rents well below market, the analysis won't tell you much.

2. If the property's expenses are too high, the gross rent multiplier does not work well. Paying the same price for a building with high expenses as one with normal expenses would be a poor investment.

3. If the property has furnished units, which usually rent for substantially more than normal rentals, the analysis would be off. Applying the same gross rent multiplier to this type of property would result in your paying a premium for used furniture and the right to pay the tenants' utilities.

So the lesson to remember is that the gross rent multiplier is only a rule of thumb; it is not nearly so accurate as the other three methods of appraisal mentioned previously, but it does provide a quick way to rank properties when you are initially looking around.

FINDING HIDDEN VALUE

Knowledge of these classic appraisal methods can be very helpful when negotiating the purchase of a property. Because most sellers list their property at or near the price they want, you need to present your lower offer with facts to back it up. If you don't, the seller may think you are trying to lowball him or her. The result could be an offer that the seller refuses to even respond to. If your offer is based on these recognized appraisal techniques, however, you have a much better chance of obtaining the property at the price you're willing to pay.

For example, assume that the owner of the duplex in Lawndale has not keep the rents up to market: let's say the rents were $1,050 (two-bedroom) and $900 (one-bedroom) for a total of $23,400 per year, definitely below market value. A well-thought-out offer would take this disparity into account. When preparing your offer, therefore, you will not only need to include an attachment with comparable sales information, but should include an estimate of the value of the property based on the capitalization-of-income method as well:

Gross Annual Income	$23,400
Less Operating Expenses	− $ 5,400
Net Income	$18,000

$18,000 (Net income) ÷ .075 (Capitalization rate)
= $240,000 (Value)

Thus, your offer of $240,000 looks reasonable. Of course, there is no guarantee the seller will take the lower offer, but at least you have a sound reason for what you consider a fair price. Especially given that the previous estimate using all three methods established a median price of $283,310, anything you can save below that price is a profit for you.

There are other ways to find such hidden profits. Let's say that your research yielded data that says that a reasonable rent for these units is $1,300 for the two-bedroom and $1,100 for the one-bedroom, giving the building a potential gross income of $28,800. The value estimate now is:

Gross Annual Income	$28,800
Less Operating Expenses	– $ 5,400
Net Income	$23,400

Therefore, using the capitalization-of-income appraisal equation, you discover that the property may actually be worth $312,000.

$$\$23,400 \text{ (Net income)} \div .075 \text{ (Capitalization rate)}$$
$$= \$312,000 \text{ (Value)}$$

Thus, you could even pay 100 percent of the asking price of $279,000 and still be secure knowing that there is upwards of $30,000 in hidden profit to be had. Yes, it will take some time to get the rents up to market levels, but once you do, the profit is yours for the taking.

THE HIGHEST AND BEST USE

Finally, one last concept you need to understand when analyzing and appraising investment property is called "highest and best use." Think about a time when you drove through a commercial area, only to see an old farm or single-family home that looked completely out of place. If you wanted to buy that property, the question is, Should it be appraised as a residence or as a commercial lot?

The answer is probably a commercial lot, for that would be the property's highest and best use.

Awareness of a building's highest and best use can yield hidden profits. Each of the following properties, for example, would warrant a valuation as its highest and best use rather than its current use:

- A house in an industrial area

- Small units on a large lot zoned for multiunits in an area with many new buildings

- Buildings that may sit on two separate lots

- An apartment house with large one-bedroom apartments that could be made into two bedrooms simply by adding a wall and a door

- A small house on a multiunit-zoned plot where extra units can be added

- A vacant commercial building that can be converted to loft apartments

Properties like these can and should be valued in more than one way. The highest and best use for the property may not be its current use. Note, however, that the highest and best use is not always obvious, as in the case of the building that sits on two lots.

The moral of the story is that real estate investing is a multidimensional task. Failure to look at all aspects may mean failure to realize the full potential of your investment. It is important to discover any hidden profits that lie waiting to be tapped.

CHAPTER 9

FINANCING REAL ESTATE

"If you would like to know the value of money, go and try to borrow some."
–BENJAMIN FRANKLIN

Locating the right financing is a critical piece to the real estate investor's puzzle. Because many of us do not have the money to purchase a property for all cash (nor should any of us preretirees want to at this point), to buy real estate we must borrow the major portion of the purchase price from a lender.

In our example property we used an FHA loan, which required only 3 percent of the purchase price as a down payment. This illustrates how even a nominal initial investment could parlay itself into a serious nest egg over time. When it comes time to buy, however, you may or may not choose to finance your properties this way. Therefore, in this chapter we'll teach you how all real estate is financed, break down the three major sources of money, and give you tips on how to find the loan that will help bring you toward the promised land of financial independence.

FIGURE 9.1
COMMON LENDING FEES

	Government Loans	Conventional Loans	Private Loans
Loan Fee (Points)	X	X	
Appraisal Fee	X	X	
Credit Report	X	X	X
Tax Service	X	X	
Document Recording	X	X	
Loan Processing	X	X	
Drawing Documents	X	X	
Funding Fee	X		
Prepaid Interest	X	X	
Mortgage Insurance	X	X	
Loan Escrow	X	X	X
Alta Title Insurance	X	X	
Setup	X	X	
Warehouse Fee	X	X	

COSTS OF BORROWING

Let's first examine the costs connected with borrowing. As you start researching loan programs, you will find that the fees associated with borrowing could vary widely. Government lending programs will charge for one thing, while conventional lenders and private parties might charge for another. Two of the greatest factors affecting your costs will be who makes the loan and what type of loan it is. The list in Figure 9.1 covers the most common fees different lending institutions may charge.

Thankfully, the federal government has taken the guesswork out of determining which fees apply when borrowing money for real estate. The governing law is the Real Estate Settlement Procedures Act (RESPA). RESPA requires that all lenders, except private parties, give borrowers an estimate of all the fees associated with their loans. Along with the RESPA estimate, the lender must also disclose the annual percentage rate (APR) of the loan. The APR will take into account all the fees that are paid on the loan up front to give a true picture of the annual interest rate that will be paid over the life of the loan.

The biggest expense is the loan fee or "points." Each point represents 1 percent of the loan amount. Points are expressed in terms of a percentage of the loan amount. For instance, if a loan costs a point and a half, this means that the cost will be 1.5 percent of the loan amount. For instance, 1.5 points on a $200,000 loan would be $3,000 in fees (1.5 × $200,000 = $3,000).

This large cash expense is a sore point for most investors. Yet, it's an integral part of the lending business and one that you will end up having to pay one way or another. This is because, for most loans, there is a normal point charge for the lender's standard rate loan. Many lenders advertise that they will make a zero-point loan. It's important to note, however, that in doing so they make up the points that they failed to charge up front by charging more interest over the life of the loan.

The best way to decide which loan program is best for you is to do an analysis of each option. Compare the cost of the zero-point, higher interest rate loan to a loan where you pay a point or two at the onset. In most cases, you will probably find that it is better to pay for the points up front than pay for them over the life of your loan.

THREE SOURCES OF MONEY

There are three primary sources to tap into when looking for a loan on residential real estate (one to four units). They are:

1. The federal government

2. Local savings and loans and banks

3. Private parties

For the remainder of this chapter, we will examine each of these money sources in detail. Let's begin by seeing how Uncle Sam is willing to help.

GOVERNMENT LENDING

As demonstrated earlier, the best source for government-supported financing for owner-occupied units is the Federal Housing Administration (FHA). Note that the FHA doesn't provide the actual funds for mortgages, but, rather, it insures home mortgage loans made by private industry lenders such as mortgage bankers, savings and loans, and banks. This insurance is necessary because FHA loans are made with such low down payment options and encouraging interest rates and terms compared with those of the conventional lending market.

The following chart illustrates the maximum loan amounts available for FHA loans in the Southern California area. These limits change depending on which region of the country you're buying in; so make sure to check with your local lender to determine the limits in your area.

Number of Units	Orange County	Los Angeles	San Diego
One	$261,609	$237,500	$261,609
Two	$334,863	$267,500	$334,054
Three	$404,724	$325,000	$404,724
Four	$502,990	$379,842	$468,300

One huge advantage of FHA loans is that they offer great leverage to the investor. With a minimum requirement of just 3 percent down, these loans can be for as much as 97 percent of the purchase price, as demonstrated with our example. Remember, however, FHA's primary objective is to encourage home ownership by first-time buyers. Therefore, one stringent requirement of the FHA program is that a buyer live in the property for a period of time as his or her primary residence. For young people this often works out great, but for those who are already established in their own homes, this particular FHA requirement may put this loan out of reach.

If you can make the move into an owner-occupied FHA loan property, however, the two- to-four unit market usually has the greatest selection of properties available, thus giving you a great chance of finding a property with a unit that will make a nice home for you and your family, plus some good income-producing units as well.

It's no secret that the American dream is to live in and own your own home. But if you can be patient, we say make your first purchase a set of FHA units. By taking advantage of the value appreciation, in a few years you could probably refinance and move up to a single-family residence. At that time you would have a house to live in as well as a nice piece of income-producing property to boot.

Besides the great leverage you can attain via an FHA loan, another advantage to buying this way is that these lenders are required to use FHA-approved appraisers. In addition to verifying the value of the building, the appraiser must make sure there are no major problems with the building and that all the basic safety measures have been met. Luckily for buyers, the guidelines for building upkeep are somewhat strict. In an instance where a building doesn't hold up to FHA standards, the seller must either comply with the appraiser's requests to fix the problems or lose the deal. Once a real estate deal has been inked, however, sellers are rarely eager to let their deal slip away. In fact, smart real estate agents will do whatever it takes to make sure their sellers comply with FHA guidelines. More often than not, sellers do comply, and by the time of closing, any deferred maintenance called out by the FHA appraiser will have been repaired.

VA LOANS AND FIRST-TIME BUYER PROGRAMS. For veterans, Uncle Sam has provided a fantastic opportunity to buy an initial set of rental units. The government's help began just after World War II. The first veterans lending program was called the GI Bill of Rights and was intended to provide war veterans with medical benefits, bonuses, and low-interest loans. VA loans are not directly made by the Department of Veterans Affairs but rather are guaranteed by it, which is similar to how FHA loans work. The great thing about GI or veterans' loans is that they can be obtained for 100 percent of the purchase price.

Finally, be sure to check out local resources, for many communities offer "first-time homebuyer" loan programs intended to help people purchase their first homes. Like FHA or VA loans, these first-time homebuyer programs usually require the property to be owner occupied yet also have low down payment options like FHA and VA loans do. Your city hall should be able to tell you if it has any such programs that would work for you. If you qualify, these kinds of programs could give you a great head start toward preparing for retirement with little money out-of-pocket.

CONVENTIONAL LOANS

Most people finance their real estate purchases through banks, savings and loans, or mortgage companies, and most of those loans are packaged using either the FNMA (Fannie Mae) or the Federal Home Loan Mortgage Corporation (Freddie Mac.) No matter what type of loan package you choose, all conventional loans fall into either one of two categories:

1. Residential loans: Residential loans are for properties that consist of either a single-family home, duplex, triplex, or fourplex.

2. Commercial loans: Commercial loans are for properties consisting of five units or more.

There are definitely major differences between these two types of loans, including the number of lenders available, qualifications, and terms. Let's look at residential loans first.

RESIDENTIAL LOANS: ONE TO FOUR UNITS. Residential loans come in unlimited forms. Here is an approximation of what you can expect.

A standard conventional loan for these smaller units is for 80 percent of the appraised value of the property. Therefore, you will have to put down 20 percent. The good news is that if you can't afford the 20 percent down, it is not impossible to structure a deal with a seller by which he or she finances a portion of it for you as a second loan. In this scenario, you, the buyer, might pay 10 percent; the seller would finance another 10 percent; and the lender would lend 80 percent (10% + 10% + 80% = 100%). Although many lenders do not allow this type of "second trust deed financing" anymore, some still do, so be sure to check out this option when shopping for a loan.

You may hear about loans that offer 90, 95, or even 100 percent financing. Yes, these loans do exist but they are usually only available for owner-occupied deals. Additionally, any loan less than 20 percent down will most likely require private mortgage insurance (PMI). PMI can be costly, but on the other hand, paying for PMI allows you to buy real estate with less than 20 percent down, so it may be worth checking out these avenues as well.

Needless to say, residential loans are based on both your creditworthiness and your ability to repay the loan. This is calculated in two ways. First, lenders will look at your FICO score, which is based on a standardized credit rating system. According to the lender, the higher your FICO score, the better risk you are. The other method of measuring your creditworthiness is by analyzing your debt-to-income ratio, which measures how much money you make versus how much you owe. After examining both of these, most lenders will end up giving you an overall creditworthiness grade of "A," "B," "C," or "D." Here is a breakdown of their criteria:

- "A" credit: Very few or no credit problems within the past two years, one or two 30-day late payments, a few small collections OK, and no more than one 30-day late payment on your mortgage.

- "B" credit: A few late payments within the past 18 months, up to four 30-day late payments or up to two 60-day late payments on revolving and installment debt, and one 90-day late payment.

- "C" credit: Many 30- to 60-day late payments in the past two years, as well as late mortgage payments in the 60- to 90-day range. Bankruptcies and foreclosures that have been discharged or settled in the past 12 months are also part of this credit rating.

- "D" credit: Open collections, charge-offs, notice of defaults, etc., as well as several missed payments, bankruptcies, and/ or foreclosures.

Of course, the lender will appraise the property in question as well, a decision that will most certainly figure into its decision to lend or not. This overall appraisal of you, your credit history, your job security, and, to a lesser extent, the property in question is what is important when applying for a loan on one to four units.

COMMERCIAL LOANS: FIVE UNITS AND UP. When the loan you want is for five units and up, you will need to apply for a commercial bank loan. Unlike residential loan lenders, the commercial loan lender primarily will consider whether the property itself can generate a profit and not depend on your personal credit history and qualifying power. Another difference between commercial loans and residential loans is that commercial loans are typically "nonrecourse" loans, in which lenders cannot come after you personally if you default; they have no recourse.

Before making a loan on five units or more, lenders will want to see that the property will generate positive cash flow. This is called "debt coverage." The debt coverage they will want is normally 1.1 to 1.25 of the monthly debt payments. This means the property must have a net cash flow, after expenses and vacancy reserves, of 1.1 to 1.25 times the loan payment. To determine the debt coverage, lenders will want to examine current rent rolls, rental history reports, and income and expense statements from at least the previous two years. To say their research will be exhaustive is an understatement.

Here is what you need to know about commercial loans:

- For loan amounts under $1 million, commercial loans will most certainly be more difficult to obtain than residential loans.

- Loan fees and interest rates are generally significantly higher than for properties in the one- to four-unit range.

- Appraisals are more extensive and cost much more than residential appraisals.

- These types of loans usually take much longer to process than loans for residential properties.

FIXED LOANS

As you likely know, two types of interest rates are available on any kind of real estate loan: fixed and adjustable rates. Many investors often prefer fixed-rate loans because they are predictable—you know exactly what you will be paying. Unfortunately, fixed-rate loans are sometimes hard to get on non-owner-occupied units.

Even so, these loans can be had. If you get a fixed-rate loan at a good rate, all the more power to you. You should know, however, a fixed-rate loan will probably be at a much higher interest rate than is an adjustable-rate loan, which will seriously cut into your cash flow. It will require higher fees, the loan won't be assumable, most will have prepayment penalties, and some have balloon payments that are due in seven to ten years. Nonetheless, when long-term interest rates are down, fixed-rate loans are highly sought after and should be considered.

ADJUSTABLE-RATE MORTGAGES. An adjustable-rate loan is one where the interest rate and payment can change as the cost of money changes for the lender. The interest rate and payment may go up and it may go down. What the rate will do actually depends on two factors: the current "index" plus the current "margin." An index is generally based on Treasury bill rates, Treasury bond rates, or the cost of money in local federal districts. A margin is a bank's cost and profit. It varies depending on market conditions and competition. The margin is the lender's profit.

You can calculate the interest rate on an adjustable-rate mortgage (ARM) loan by using the following formula:

Current rate of index + Margin of loan = Interest rate

For example, if the index is 4.89 and the margin is 2.35, you can calculate the interest on an ARM as follows:

4.92% Rate + 2.35% Margin = 7.27% Interest rate

There are essentially two types of adjustable-rate mortgage loans:

1. "No-neg" adjustables: No-neg adjustables are loans that do not allow for any negative amortization.

2. "Neg-am" adjustables: Neg-am adjustables are loans that do allow for negative amortization.

What is negative amortization? In simple terms, if your monthly payment on your adjustable-rate mortgage is $875, but it would take $925 a month to pay off the loan in 30 years, then $50 a month (the difference between $875 and $925) can be added to the loan balance. That is negative amortization.

The "no-neg" is an adjustable loan with terms that do not allow potential negative amortization. In guaranteeing that there will be no negative amortization, the lender builds in protection for potential interest-rate increases. To do that, most allow for two interest adjustments each year, one every six months. The maximum increase in the interest rate is usually 1 percent each period with a corresponding adjustment in the payment. For this maximum increase, the bank will absorb any increase above the 2 percent (1 percent every six months) increase per year.

The "neg-am" loan differs by limiting how much your payment can increase rather than how much the interest can increase. Payment caps on neg-am loans are usually set at a maximum of 7.5 percent increase per year. For example, on a loan payment of $1,500 per month, a 7.5 percent increase in payment is $112.50 per month ($1,500.00 × .075 = $112.50). To compensate the lenders for the lower payment, the interest rate is allowed to adjust every month according to the index it is tied to. With this type of loan, going negative will be an option you can choose, or not choose, each month. This is because the lender gives you different payment options each time it sends a bill. For this reason, this loan is sometimes rightfully called the "flexible payment plan loan."

People complain that with neg-am adjustable loans, loan balances can increase rather than decrease. Of course this can happen. But in reality this is a psychological problem and not a practical one. Why is it that we can finance a brand-new car, knowing full well that the loan will be larger than the car's value the moment we drive it off the lot? And everyone knows that the computer systems we buy today will be behind the times in less than six months, but we continue to buy new computer systems all the time. In truth, we buy new cars and computers on credit because they enhance the quality of our lives. Using neg-am adjustable loans to purchase the real estate that will help us retire in style one day should be no different. Keep in mind that lending is just a tool to help you reach your dreams. If a neg-am adjustable loan is the tool that will work for you, then by all means consider this option.

For the conservative investor who is working out a 10- to 20-year retirement plan, the fixed-rate loan is probably best, that is, if the numbers work out so the property makes sense with the fixed rate. For many younger investors, the lower start rates on the adjustable loans may be the only way to buy. In that case, stick a bumper sticker on your car that says ADJUSTABLE-RATE MORTGAGE OR BUST, and go for it.

Regardless of the type of conventional loan you choose, it is important that you shop around for the best possible terms. As you can see, many variables will affect your costs. Use the following uniform checklist to compare programs effectively:

- Interest rate

- Fixed or adjustable

- Loan-to-value ratio

- Debt coverage percentage

- Points

- Appraisal fee

- Environmental review fee

- Margin

- Index

- Interest rate cap

- Payment cap

- Required impounds

- Prepayment penalty

- Yield maintenance

- Recourse or nonrecourse

- Processing time

- Good-faith deposit

- Other fees

ASSUMABLE LOANS. As the name implies, assumable loans are loans already in place that can be assumed by the person purchasing the property. Rather than finding new financing and paying all the corresponding fees, assumable loans allow a buyer to pay a small fee, usually one point, and take over someone else's existing loan.

Assumable loans are a great option because they often offer better terms than similar new loans. Perhaps interest rates were better at the time an original loan was put on the property. If so, a purchaser who takes over a loan like this would make out great.

Additionally, after an assumable loan has been in place for many years, it starts paying off the principal at a rapid clip. For an investor preparing for retirement, an assumable loan makes sense because it may allow you to get a loan that will often be paid off in full near the time you retire. There is nothing as comforting as starting retirement with a piece of income property that is paid off in full. Talk about cash flow!

PRIVATE-PARTY FINANCING

The last source of real estate funding is through private-party financing. These loans are usually made by the sellers of the property themselves wanting to take advantage of installment sales and offer several advantages over conventional loans. First of all, by obtaining some private-party financing you can save a lot of money in lending fees, for most of the costs associated with conventional financing do not apply to private loans. Second, because this is a private contract, the buyer and seller can create whatever win-win terms they want to make the deal work.

It may surprise you to learn that many sellers who offer private financing do not want any down payment at all. Instead of a big lump-sum down payment, which actually can be a tax headache for them, these sellers/financers are looking for monthly income from carrying the paper as illustrated a few chapters back when we discussed tax planning. Many of these sellers only want enough money down to pay the closing costs. After that, the income you will provide them is just gravy.

So the rule is this: Anything goes. A contract is like your own private set of laws, and the two parties to that contract can create whatever "laws" (terms) work for them. Many sellers may offer financing at lower interest rates than the going conventional rate and may also offer payment terms to fit most needs. In fact, it is not unusual for sellers to carry long-term financing with interest-only payments. Why? Because they make more money, that's why. Again, the situation becomes win-win for everybody. In fact, we have seen many transactions in which the payments were lower than interest-only in order to wrap up the deal. Usually, it is because a seller has not kept the rents up with the market, and thus a graduated payment schedule allows the buyer to raise rents over time.

The last thing to consider when looking at a private-party loan is the paid-in-full due date. As with a conventional loan, it can be 1 year, 5 years, or 30 years, whatever you agree on. You should not be surprised if the seller wants to set up some partial lump-sum pay-offs at preset times. The seller may have loans it needs to pay off down the road or may want to pay for the college education for a grandchild, for example. In these situations, the seller should allow you to get the funds by refinancing the property and putting its loan in the second position.

Another type of private lending is the "land sale contract," or "contract for deed." Here, the actual title to the property does not transfer at the time of the loan. Instead, the seller keeps the title in his or her name until the loan is paid off. Deals are often structured this way to help the buyer qualify. This is not unlike a car loan, where the lender keeps the title until the car is paid off in full.

One final source for private financing is known as the "hard-money market." Intended for the difficult-to-qualify buyer, hard-money loans are made by third parties at high interest rates. This may be due to the buyer's poor credit or because the property is in bad shape. Just know that hard-money loans are available for those deals that cannot get financed conventionally.

TO SUM UP

Financing is a tool to accomplish your goals. Try to avoid getting worked up over the minute details of the loan. Find a property that fits your goals, and a loan that allows you to accomplish those goals, and be happy. Remember that other options like assumable financing, land sale contracts, and hard-money lending are all available to complete the deal, and that is what you want.

CHAPTER 10

MINDING
THE FARM

"Treat your customers like human beings—and they will always come back."
—L.L. BEAN

The day you close escrow on a piece of property is the day the real work of being a real estate investor begins. It's now time to take over managing your building and to start running your new real estate business in earnest. Certainly, closing that first escrow and taking on a challenge such as this can be an intimidating, if not a terrifying, proposition. Especially when you think of dealing with the new mortgage you'll need to meet, ill-timed vacancies, and the thought of listening to tenants complaining about barking dogs and clogged toilets. Thankfully, with a little bit of study and practice, you can learn the skills necessary to handle all these kinds of issues— and then some.

In this chapter we offer some key lessons in property management. Our goal is to help you get a jump start on taking over your building with total and complete confidence.

OPEN FOR BUSINESS

Simplistic as it may sound, this really is a people business. Some real estate investors tend to focus on the money they're going to make and forget that you make the money by keeping the customer content. In this instance, the customer is your tenant. If you keep your tenants content, they will eventually reward you in kind. Namely, with their help, you will someday soon be able to retire in style.

The first order of business once you close on any purchase will be to meet and greet the tenants you just inherited. Either post notes on their doors or mail them letters introducing yourself as the new owner. Let the tenants know that you would like to meet them personally and that you will be calling in a day or so to set up a convenient time to do so. Your goal is to meet them, answer any questions they may have, and, most important, get a new rental agreement filled out with both of your signatures on it.

When it comes to rental agreements, it would be wise not to use those preprinted ones that are available at your local stationery store. These all-purpose rental agreements are usually very general and lack the specific details necessary to protect you in case of a dispute. On the other hand, we do recommend that you use rental agreements that you can obtain from your local apartment owners' association. These agreements are usually written by lawyers who specialize in landlord/tenant law and will contain all the necessary standard clauses to protect both you and your tenants.

Should you go with month-to-month agreements or leases? When you first take over the reins of control, the decision won't be up to you, because you will be obligated to honor the previous agreements that you inherited. Once the terms of those agreements are met, however, the decision becomes all yours. You will find that local custom will often dictate what kinds of tenancies are standard in your area. In some communities, month-to-month agreements are preferred. In others, leases are the most common. In short, month-to-month agreements allow landlords and tenants to terminate the agreement with just 30 to 60 days' notice. Leases, on the other hand, lock both parties in at an agreed-on rental rate for an extended period of time (usually one year for residential income property). Therefore, the type of tenancies that you choose will ultimately depend on the amount of flexibility you desire.

When meeting the tenants for the first time you should also be prepared with any other necessary agreements that need signatures. At some properties, especially larger multiunit buildings, tenants must agree to a list of house rules. This list may include rules such as "No loud music after 9 PM" or "Please clean up after yourself in the laundry room." If you want to run a tight ship, this is something you might consider, too. Additionally, you may have a duty to inform your tenants of any hazardous materials that might be on the property. California and New York, for example, have required disclosures regarding lead-based paint and other environmental concerns that tenants need to be made aware of.

Finally, you should provide an interior inspection checklist for review by the tenant and you or your property manager. On taking ownership, walk the unit with your tenant and go over the following checklist together. When finished, make sure you both sign and date it. This will eliminate most disagreements over deposit refunds in the event you need to charge the tenants because of any material damage they did to the unit.

Interior Inspection Checklist:

- Condition of carpet

- Condition of vinyl and other floor coverings

- Condition of paint

- Holes in walls

- Condition of ceilings

- List of landlord-owned appliances and their condition

- Condition of doors, windows, and window screens

- Condition of garage, carport, and/or storage area

- List of keys and accessories

- Anything else you can think of

There are both benefits and risks to getting to know your tenants personally. For the most part, you should keep your contact with the tenants on a strictly business level. Sure, it's OK to be friendly with your tenants, but being friends with them should be something you should consider carefully. By keeping things on a business level you can ask for the rent guiltfree, even if you know their kids have been sick or their spouses got laid off from their jobs.

Protecting your privacy should be of paramount importance to you. Here are a few things you can do to ensure your privacy:

- Never give out your home address to your tenants or your resident manager.

- Never give out your home phone number to your tenants.

- Have your home phone number unlisted.

- Get the caller ID feature added to your phone service.

- Pick up the rent in person or have it mailed to a post office box or other place of business. Do not have the rent mailed to your house.

- Set up a post office box before you buy any piece of property. This way, your address will not show up on any utility bills or public documents.

- Get either a voice mail service or a pager to answer any calls that come in from ads or tenants regarding your property. Thus, you are available for emergencies but can still protect your privacy.

When you get a new agreement signed, discuss with the tenants how and when you want rent paid. If it is a common practice in your area for the rent to be paid at the beginning of the month, then that should be your policy, too. However, you may end up making some concessions on this issue, especially if the tenants you inherited had different arrangements with the former owner because of payday issues. If you decide that you would like to keep these tenants for a while, you might consider honoring their former arrangements. You probably won't lose anything, and will, alternatively, create some goodwill between you and your new tenants.

Now that you're in business for yourself you'll also need a policy about accepting personal checks for rent payment. Unfortunately, tenants' rent checks sometimes bounce, and if they do, you are the one who will be affected. Sometimes it's on purpose; most often, it's not. Nonetheless, you should have a strict rule that if a tenant's rent check bounces, you can no longer accept personal checks from him or her. Furthermore, in the future the tenant must pay the rent with either a cashier's check or a money order. Additionally, you should not allow your tenants to pay their rent in cash. Besides the inherent accounting problem it poses, accepting cash can make you an easy target for a robbery.

HUD HOUSING

Because many people cannot afford adequate housing, the government has created several assistance programs to help these people. The most common is through the Department of Housing and Urban Development (HUD). HUD's original goal dates back to the Housing Act of 1949. The purpose of this law was to provide "a decent home and a suitable living environment for every American family."

The program under which this rental-payment assistance is administered is called Section 8. Some cities receive Section 8 assistance and others maintain offices that administer housing assistance programs via vouchers. If qualified for either of these programs, the applicants will have part of their rent paid by the government, while they will be responsible for the balance. In most cases the tenant's share of the rent does not exceed 20 percent to 30 percent of his or her monthly income. As you can see, the advantage of having Section 8 or voucher tenants is that it makes decent homes affordable to a larger section of the population. What's more, the majority of their rent is paid for by the government, and, thankfully, Uncle Sam almost always pays on time.

Part of the job of HUD is to ascertain the general market rent for various size apartments and houses in the community. This rent schedule becomes the top rent the tenants are able to pay, including any subsidies by HUD. What's great is that if you have rentals in an area with HUD subsidies, you may find the rent HUD sets to be more than reasonable. These rental rates are based on the size of the unit, utilities paid, appliances provided, condition of the neighborhood, and so on.

One hurdle you will need to face with a HUD-assisted tenant is the inspection of your property by a HUD official. HUD's goal is to provide decent, safe, and sanitary conditions for the tenants. As long as the apartment passes the yearly HUD inspection, it will pass the program's requirements. If so, as a landlord, you could benefit for years to come with rental rates at, or above, the top of the market.

DISCRIMINATION

Regardless of whether you are the resident-manager of a 50-unit apartment complex or the owner of a few modest two- and three-unit buildings, federal antidiscrimination laws now apply to you, as may a number of state and local ordinances. The federal Civil Rights Act and Fair Housing Act prohibit landlords from discriminating on the basis of race, ethnic background, national origin, religion, and sex. The Americans with Disabilities Act (ADA) effectively prohibits discrimination against someone with a disability.

When it comes to picking new tenants, the law says that if you are faced with two equally qualified tenants, it is OK to pick one over another for no other reason than you liked one better; there is nothing discriminatory in that. If you have a pattern of not choosing women, African-Americans, Jews, or other minorities, however, you leave yourself open to what could be an expensive discrimination lawsuit.

Even if you are not discriminating when renting your units, you should be just as concerned with the appearance of discrimination. For example, your apartment building may be occupied only by young white urban professionals. In this instance, you may appear to be discriminating, even if you are not. The key to minimizing that risk is to set up some objective, legitimate business criteria when looking for new tenants and adhere to them. The law says that you must treat all applicants equally, so use the same criteria in every case. Look consistently for such things as three personal references, a steady employment history, and good credit. Write down your criteria and keep it on file. Most important, be consistent, and document your grounds for denying someone an apartment.

UTILITIES AND INSURANCE

During escrow, you should have found out who the local utility companies are and who does the regular maintenance work on your building. Now that you are the new owner you will have to transfer all these services to your name. The local utility companies might also want deposits or to run credit checks for your new service. Make sure you handle these issues well in advance of closing. It would make a poor first impression on your tenants if the utilities were shut off the very day you took over.

When it comes to insurance, you were probably required by your lender to purchase some for your building before you ever closed escrow. This insurance covered you and the lender in case of fire. But what about insurance for the manager and the workers that come onto the property to work? Getting some insurance to cover them might be a wise idea as well. You may not think you have any employees for your modest triplex, but perhaps you do: The kid who cuts your grass, the plumber who fixes the leaky faucets in the bathrooms, and the tenant who shows the vacant unit for you, will all probably be considered employees by a court of law if they get injured while working on your property. Thus, you should find out if your existing policy covers these casual workers. If not, you need to get a policy to cover them.

One way around having to buy another pricey insurance policy would be to use contractors who can prove they have their own workers' compensation insurance before they do any work for you. Self-insured contractors, however, usually charge much more than the casual local handyman does, because these contractors have to pay all their own fees and obtain all the licenses for the work they do.

THE APARTMENT OWNERS ASSOCIATION

Now that you're a landlord, you should join your local apartment owners association. You can locate one easy enough by searching through the National Apartment Association offices by state in the Appendix, looking in the yellow pages, via the Internet, or by contacting your state department of real estate. If, for some reason, there isn't one in your own community, try to find an apartment owners association in the nearest major city to you and join that group.

Why is an apartment owners association so important to join? These organizations are usually run by experienced apartment owners and professional property managers. Their purpose is to help other owners and managers. Most provide monthly newsletters, which will keep you up-to-date on current events, local laws and relevant ordinances, rental rates, and any changes taking place in your market. They also carry advertisements for plumbers, roofers, electricians, and others who can help you when you need it. In addition, many associations will supply you with various forms you might need, including the types of rental agreements mentioned earlier. Some even are able to run credit checks on any potential new tenants you may have.

WHO'S DOING WHAT?

It's important for you to stay current on what's happening in your neighborhood. You probably did some initial investigation before you bought your property, but now you need to keep an ongoing log about the neighborhood and the buildings that surround yours. Some of the things to note in your landlord's notebook would include:

- Number of units in the surrounding buildings

- Number of properties on the streets

- Phone numbers from the For Rent signs

- Amenities in the other properties

- Rental rates and terms on the vacancies

- Overall condition of the streets

- Location and phone numbers of local police and fire departments

This isn't a project that you should begin and finish in one day. Rather, it will be an ongoing process for as long as you are building your nest egg through real estate. And because this is a working notebook, it doesn't have to be fancy. You want to use it to keep track of the facts you learn about the streets and buildings that surround your property over the long haul. The primary goal of your notes is to get a broad overview of what's happening at all times. These notes will help you make decisions about your property in the future.

DETERMINING VACANCY RATES

You'll notice that the first item on the preceding list was to find out how many units are in the surrounding buildings. By knowing how many units are out there you can determine your neighborhood's vacancy rate and thus will be able to monitor changes in vacancy trends.

There is a fast and easy way to determine your local vacancy rate. To begin with, just count the number of mailboxes that you see in your neighborhood. It is not necessary that you be 100 percent accurate, for you just want an estimate of how many units there are. Once you know the number of units, you can estimate the vacancy rate by counting the number of For Rent signs in that same area and then dividing that number by the number of mailboxes. The math will look like this:

Number of FOR RENT signs ÷ Number of mailboxes = Vacancy rate

This method of determining the vacancy rate is an inexact science, but it should help you determine a general vacancy rate at a given time. With this knowledge at your fingertips you will always be able to stay one step ahead of the competition.

DETERMINING RENTAL RATES

Because the thought of managing your units on your own may give you initial pause, odds are you're considering turning your buildings over to professional management right after you purchase them. No doubt about it, though, it is best to get your feet wet by managing your first buildings yourself—your bottom-line return will be significantly better and you will be much wiser from this experience. But managing your own units isn't always practical for every investor and you may have no choice but to use professional management. One way to double-check your management company's effectiveness is to "manage the manager." You can do this by always knowing what the market rate for rent should be via a simple rent survey that you conduct yourself.

It is easy to do a rent survey. One good way is to pretend you are a prospective tenant. Whenever you see a FOR RENT sign in your neighborhood, jot down the phone number and call on the unit. Make sure you ask all the applicable questions that any prospective tenant would and then note the details in your notebook.

Rental survey questions:

- How much is the unit renting for?

- How many bedrooms and bathrooms does the unit have?

- What is the square footage of the apartment?

- What amenities are included?

- Do they accept pets?

- Will it be a month-to-month agreement or a lease?

- How much will it cost to move in?

- Can you see the inside of the unit?

By habitually doing this exercise, you will accumulate plenty of ammunition to guard yourself against a complacent management company. It is very easy for a management company to produce good numbers if it never pushes the rents to the upper end of the market. But this is a business, and your cash-on-cash return and nest egg depend on management keeping the rental rate at the correct level. Your tenants will never moan if your rents are too low; in fact, they'll be thrilled and probably will never move. But keep in mind that when it comes time to refinance or sell, any lower-than-market rental rates will directly affect the value of your building.

FILLING A VACANCY

As a real estate investor, you will wear many different hats. The very day a tenant tells you that he or she is moving is the day you put on your salesperson's hat; it's now time to market your vacant apartment to someone new. The key to getting your apartment filled as quickly as possible lies in doing the right kind of advertising for your soon-to-be-vacant apartment. Some of the best advertising methods are:

- Place a rental sign or banner out front.

- Offer a referral fee to an existing tenant.

- Hold open houses on weekends.

- Post flyers at local businesses.

- Place ads in the local newspapers.

- Send direct-mail material to tenants in similar buildings.

- Register with rental agencies.

- Contract with management company.

Your decision on how much or how little advertising you will need to do will be based on the results of your ongoing vacancy surveys. Normally, the lower the vacancy rate, the quicker the unit will fill and the less effort is needed to fill it. Most important is that you get the unit filled so you don't lose any rent. Remember, if you wait to advertise your vacancy until the current tenant leaves, you will probably lose a month's rent.

The secret to not having any downtime is to start your advertising campaign the day you receive notice from the tenant that he or she is moving. Even if the rental market is strong and you only need a FOR RENT sign to attract someone new, put it up right away. The sooner your unit is on the market, the better chance you have to get the best selection of future tenants. You don't just want a replacement tenant; you want the best-qualified tenant who is willing to pay you for your vacancy immediately.

Most landlords drop the ball when it comes to rerenting a unit by not getting the unit cleaned and "rent-ready" in a timely manner. One key to not falling into this trap is finding out ahead of time what has to be done and lining up the proper contractors to do the work. When a tenant gives notice, you or your manager should meet with the tenant and walk through the unit to see what needs to be done to clean it up and get it ready for someone new. Things like tired carpet, scuffed walls, ripped screens, and so on should be written down on a fix-it list.

Once you have a list to work from, you can schedule the work so it can be finished in a timely manner. In most instances, many small items may need to be replaced that you can buy ahead of time—things like towel bars, shower curtains, window coverings, light fixtures, and so on. The goal is to get the unit completely finished as quickly as possible, whether or not you have a new tenant ready to move in.

Two points to remember are:

1. If you have a tenant ready to move in, he or she usually wants to move in as soon as possible, so get the unit rent-ready as quickly as you can.

2. If you don't have a tenant lined up, it is easier to rent a unit that is clean and ready to move into.

A POLICY ON PETS

When you buy your building you will inherit a pet policy from the previous owner; he or she either allowed pets or didn't. Now that the building is under your watch, should you consider renting your units to tenants with pets? Don't say no so fast. Here are some reasons we say yes to pets:

- You can command a premium rent from someone with a pet.

- Because most landlords don't allow pets, it's difficult for someone with a pet to find a new residence. By considering these tenants, you will have a large pool of grateful tenants to pick from.

- Because it's so difficult for pet owners to find an apartment that allows pets, pet owners generally stay in the apartment longer than nonpet owners do.

- Most pet owners will be willing to put down a large security deposit if you accept them as a tenant. If the pet damages the apartment, you will have the money to fix it and make it as good as new for the next tenant.

- Accepting tenants with pets is a good method of combating periods of high vacancy.

As you can see, there are plenty of good reasons why you may want to accept tenants with pets—all of them financial. If you do decide to consider pets, you should advertise your unit just that way: "Will consider small pets, call to discuss." Make sure you interview the pet as well as the tenant. A dog that yips and barks would be a bad idea, but one that is generally quiet or a cat that is litter box-trained might be perfectly OK.

HAPPY TENANTS

This chapter began with a quote from L.L. Bean talking about the importance of keeping your customers happy. As mentioned, your customers are your tenants, and making sure they get their money's worth for the dollars they pay in rent is a key component to your ultimate success. This is the basic philosophy most businesses operate under, but when it come to renting apartments, this sometimes becomes easy to forget.

Lots of investors buy a building or two, fix them up, and fill them with nice new tenants. Unfortunately, as the years go on, they often let their buildings deteriorate. But this doesn't have to happen. If you want to have a sharp building with a great tenant base, fix it up, manage it properly, and keep up the property at all times. This will ensure two things:

1. The current tenants will want to stay in the nice home you helped create for them.

2. Prospective tenants will see how you care for the building and will be willing to pay you top dollar to live there.

Remember that most restaurant customers don't complain about bad food, they just don't come back. With units, if you let the building deteriorate without keeping it up, the tenants will probably just find another place to live rather than complain to a deaf ear.

It's important to take care of tenant requests as fast as possible. The truth is that most people don't like to complain, so when they do, assume that the problem has been going on long enough that it is really starting to be a nuisance. You should also get in the habit of asking your tenants how things are going in the building whenever you see them. They may forget to mention that little leak under their sink unless you ask. On the other hand, by finding out about small problems early on you can nip bigger problems in the bud. The end result will always be more money in your pocket.

RAISING THE RENT

Raising rents is always a sensitive issue with landlords and tenants alike. The trouble with many small property owners is they get friendly with their tenants. As mentioned, being friends with your tenants just makes asking for more rent that much harder. But the bottom line is that this is a business, and your cash-on-cash return and your building's ultimate value depend on your rental rate. Therefore, raising rents periodically is part of the deal. Your tenants know it and now so do you.

The first secret to raising rents successfully is to know what the other owners in your neighborhood are getting for comparable units. If they are getting more than you are, then a rent increase for your units is probably in order. Many landlords fear that their tenants will move out if they raise the rents. The truth, however, is that most people won't go to the trouble and expense of moving just to "get even" with their landlord. Explain to your tenants that you are forced to give them a cost-of-living increase and are only taking the rent to the new market rate for the area. Your tenants certainly will not be happy about it, but if you've made a strong case about what market rents are, then there really isn't too much they can do about it. In a worst-case scenario, your tenant may give you notice and move out. In that instance, get the unit rent ready as soon as possible and charge the next tenant the market rent you deserve.

To soften the blow of a rent increase, consider doing something extra for your tenants. It doesn't hurt to follow or precede a cost-of-living increase with some upgrades to the building. You might consider putting some new plants or flowers in front of the building or new doormats in front of the apartments. Another idea would be to have all the outside windows washed at your expense. Even a $15 gift certificate to their local Starbucks would remind them how lucky they are to have you as their landlord.

One great way to get the message out to your tenants about rents in an increasing market is to prominently display the current rental rate on your FOR RENT signs. When your existing tenants see your other units being rented at a much higher rate for anyone new coming in, they will be far less apt to object when they get a raise, especially if they are paying less than market rent.

CONCLUSION

We've covered a lot of information in this book. If we did our job right, you should be plenty worried about your prospects in retirement. On the other hand, our hope is that you have been moved enough by our message so that you will take a positive step to find a better way to fund your future.

A mentor of ours has always preached, "If you always do what you've always done, you'll always get what you always got." Truer words couldn't be spoken, especially for the 95 percent of American retirees who retire practically broke. To add insult to injury, the amount of money needed to retire comfortably is increasing, and the effects of inflation often hit retirees the hardest. The good news is that medical advances are giving all of us the possibility of many more years of a healthy life after retirement. The question is, If you're practically broke when you do retire, is that really good news?

Most of us probably never gave it much thought when we started our careers, but work is something we'll be doing for 30 to

40 years of our lives. While working we honorably and consistently pay into Social Security, or maybe even a company pension plan, all with the expectation that those investments would magically pay off as they were supposed to. As the future of Social Security grows ever dimmer, however, and the Enron debacle proves, to think we'll be taken care of in retirement by others is nothing but a pipe dream.

To solve this dilemma we haven't suggested any major life-changing moves. Instead, one solution is to not fall for the Social Security/401(k)/pension fund hocus-pocus trap. As you know, there's no way those things will fill the bill when your time comes. Another solution is to refuse to abdicate the responsibility for your retirement by turning it over to experts picked by the people that are "supposed to know." If they really knew, the 95 percentile statistic wouldn't be what it is.

No, you need to take charge of this most important issue for yourself and make concrete plans now to create a worthwhile nest egg later. We say do it via real estate, or do it any other way that works, but above all just do it so you don't have to work forever. Of course, you know that we believe real estate is the best and safest way. Our challenge has been to lay out the facts so that you believe it, too. The limited space in this book has only allowed us to touch the high points of investing in real estate. This review should have given you an outline of the topics that need additional study and research.

We encourage you to use the five-part system we laid out in Chapter 4. Remember, we're talking about a process that will pay off in 15 to 30 years. We want you to get started, but, as important, get started on the right foot. To recap, the components of the system are:

1. **Learn** about real estate as an investment vehicle.

2. **Research** property in your local market.

3. **Plan** how to invest your money.

4. **Invest** your funds according to your plan.

5. **Manage** your property according to your plan.

We realize how hard it will be for many of you to get started. There are always people around who will tell you why it won't work. They will fill you with fear about property management and tell you how their uncle or family friend lost everything trying to do just what you're contemplating doing. But these are the people who will be in that 95 percentile practically broke group. That is, unless they hit the lottery, which, of course, they play every week. What we hope you have learned is that we're not talking about a system of winning by chance like the lottery. We're talking about a system of investing based on education—your education.

Our approach in this book has been to present an ultraconservative approach to this topic—that is, buy a property or two with the goal of getting them paid off by the time you retire. This simple plan should make a significant difference in your life in retirement. What makes this approach tough to sell is that it takes 15 to 30 years to see the real payoff. On the other hand, it's a lot easier to motivate people with dreams of the get-rich-quick approaches to making money—things like "placing tiny little ads in papers" to sell things or buying and flipping distressed real estate for nothing down. Sure, these ideas do work out sometimes, but more often than not, people flock to them too quickly and the inherent pitfalls in these ideas swallow them whole.

Odds are if you accept your probable fate for your future, you are on the road to a better way to care for you and your family. No doubt that a modest investment in real estate now could allow you to have the fruitful future you have dreamed of. For many, getting started small will lead to greater investments and bigger rewards— rewards beyond their wildest expectations. But let's not get ahead of ourselves. Never forget that the number one goal is to provide financial security for your retirement. Anything beyond that is gravy.

You'll remember that we began each chapter of this book with a phrase or quote. Some were famous, some were catchy, some poignant, some funny, some not. As we get older we learn what's behind people saying such things; it's usually because their words convey a hard-earned truth. In most cases, it's easier to make a change when you personally experience the truth of one of these sayings. The truth of the topic of our book—retirement—isn't as forgiving.

We have a framed golf print in the lobby of our office. Below a silhouette of a golfer making a perfect back swing, the print reads, "In the game of life play well, you don't get a second round." It's an interesting saying to put under a golfer because in some golf games there is such a thing as a "mulligan." A mulligan is a friendly unwritten rule that allows a player to take a bad shot over with no penalty. The idea is that the golfer'll hopefully do a better job the next time he or she swings the club.

Because you don't get a mulligan in the game of life, all we ask is that you take our message seriously and do it differently than the rest.

NATIONAL APARTMENT ASSOCIATION OFFICES BY STATE

Alabama

Alabama Apartment Association
2806 Artie St., Suite 3
Huntsville, AL 35805
Phone: 800-318-8785
Fax: 256-539-6311

Apartment Association of the
   Tennessee Valley, Inc.
2806 Artie St.
Huntsville, AL 35805
Phone: 256-539-2998
Fax: 256-539-6311

Birmingham Apartment Association
1553 Deer Valley Dr.
Birmingham, AL 35226
Phone: 205-989-5785
Fax: 205-426-7919
Web site: <www.birminghamapart
   mentassociation.com>

Mobile Bay Area Apartment Association
255 St. Francis St.
Mobile, AL 36602
Phone: 334-626-7142
Fax: 334-666-4220

Montgomery Apartment Association
P.O. Box 11493
Mobile, AL 36111
Phone: 334-213-7307
Fax: 334-260-0665

Alaska

National Apartment Association
201 North Union St., Suite 200
Alexandria, VA 22314
Phone: 703-518-6141

Arizona

National Apartment Association
201 North Union St., Suite 200
Alexandria, VA 22314
Phone: 703-518-6141

Arkansas

Arkansas Apartment Association
P.O. Box 250273
Little Rock, AR 72225
Phone: 501-664-8300
Fax: 501-664-0927
Web site: <www.arapartments.com>

Arkansas Multi-Family Housing
  Association
P.O. Box 250313
Little Rock, AR 72225
Phone: 501-312-3055
Fax: 501-604-2678
Web site: <www.arapartments.com>

Northwest Arkansas Apartment
  Association
1916 South 9th St., #143
Rogers, AR 72758-6370
Phone: 479-621-8236
Fax: 479-621-8239
Web site: <www.nwaaa.biz>

California

National Apartment Association
201 North Union St., Suite 200
Alexandria, VA 22314
Phone: 703-518-6141

Colorado

Apartment Association of Metro Denver
650 S. Cherry St., #635
Denver, CO 80246
Phone: 303-329-3300
Fax: 303-329-0403
Web site: <www.aamdhq.org>

Apartment Association of Colorado
  Springs
888 Garden of the Gods Rd., Suite 103
Colorado Springs, CO 80907
Phone: 719-264-9195
Fax: 719-264-9198
Web site: <www.aacshq.org>

Boulder County Apartment Association
P.O. Box 17606
Boulder, CO 80308
Phone: 303-449-9048
Fax: 303-449-7028

CAA–Fort Collins Chapter
P.O. Box 1075
Fort Collins, CO 80522
Phone: 970-223-0545
Fax: 970-223-4541
Web site: <www.fortcollins-rentals.net>

Colorado Apartment Association
650 S. Cherry St., #635
Denver, CO 80246
Phone: 303-329-3300
Fax: 303-329-0403

Pueblo Apartment Association
P.O. Box 987
Pueblo, CO 81002
Phone: 719-584-2121
Fax: 719-584-2204

Weld County Apartment Association
P.O. Box 1418
Greeley, CO 80632
Phone: 970-352-1608
Fax: 970-353-0325

Connecticut

Connecticut Apartment Association
41 Crossroads Plaza #141
W. Hartford, CT 06117
Phone: 203-554-2822
Fax: 860-953-9719
Web site: <www.ctaahq.org>

Delaware

Delaware Apartment Association
799 Montclair Dr., #4
Claymont, DE 19703-3625
Phone: 302-798-0635
Fax: 302-798-1726

District of Columbia

Apartment & Office Building
  Association (AOBA)
1050 17th St., NW, #300
Washington, DC 20036
Phone: 202-296-3390
Fax: 202-296-3399

Florida

Apartment Association of Greater
  Orlando
340 North Maitland Ave.
Maitland, FL 32751
Phone: 407-644-0539
Fax: 407-644-6288
Web site: <www.aago.org>

Bay Area Apartment Association
4509 George Rd.
Tampa, FL 33634
Phone: 813-882-0222
Fax: 813-884-0326

Bay County Multi-Housing Association
P.O. Box 16686
Panama City, FL 32406
Phone: 850-763-5522

Capital City Apartment Association
431 Waverly Rd.
Tallahassee, FL 32312
Phone: 850-531-0628
Fax: 850-531-0628

Florida Apartment Association
1133 West Morse Blvd., Suite 201
Winter Park, FL 32789
Phone: 407-647-8839
Fax: 407-629-2502
Web site: <www.fl-apartments.org>

Gainesville Apartment Association
P.O. Box 140926
Gainesville, FL 32614
Phone: 352-335-1800
Fax: 352-335-1800

Jacksonville Apartment Association
3047-1 St. Johns Bluff Rd. South
Jacksonville, FL 32246
Phone: 904-997-1890
Fax: 904-997-1891

Naples Area Apartment Association
P.O. Box 990028
Naples, FL 34116
Phone: 941-455-6663
Fax: 941-455-9567

South East Florida Apartment
  Association
1650 S. Dixie Hwy, Suite 500
Boca Raton, FL 33432
Phone: 561-447-0696
Fax: 561-395-8557
Web site: <www.sefaa.com>

Southwest Florida Apartment
  Association
P.O. Box 61933
Fort Myers, FL 33907
Phone: 941-338-6055
Fax: 941-275-0504

Space Coast Apartment Association
c/o SCPM, 1617 Cooling Ave.
Melbourne, FL 32935
Phone: 321-757-9609
Fax: 321-757-9597

Tri-City Apartment Association
4509 George Rd.
Tampa, FL 33634
Phone: 800-276-1927
Fax: 813-884-0326

Georgia

Athens Apartment Association
P.O. Box 7086
Athens, GA 30604
Phone: 706-549-8888
Fax: 706-549-3304

Atlanta Apartment Association
8601 Dunwoody Pl., Suite 318
Atlanta, GA 30350
Phone: 770-518-4248
Fax: 770-518-4373
Web site: <www.atl-apt.org>

C.S.R.A. Apartment Association
P.O. Box 211325
Martinez, GA 30917-1325
Phone: 706-868-9567
Fax: 706-866-4949

Columbus Apartment Association
P.O. Box 8986
Columbus, GA 31909
Phone: 706-653-2024
Fax: 706-653-2203

Georgia Apartment Association
8601 Dunwoody Pl., Suite 318
Atlanta, GA 30350
Phone: 770-518-4248
Fax: 770-518-4373
Web site: <www.ga-apt.org>

Mid Georgia Apartment Association
P.O. Box 18184
Macon, GA 31209
Phone: 478-994-8773
Fax: 478-994-8774

North Georgia Apartment Association
P.O. Box 200535
Cartersville, GA 30120
Phone: 770-386-2921
Fax: 770-386-1937

Savannah Apartment Association
P.O. Box 13247
Savannah, GA 31416
Phone: 912-920-3207
Fax: 912-920-3207
Web site: <www.savaptassoc.org>

Hawaii

National Apartment Association
201 North Union St., Suite 200
Alexandria, VA 22314
Phone: 703-518-6141

Idaho

Idaho Rental Owners & Managers
    Association
P.O. Box 15393
Boise, ID 83715-5393
Phone: 208-336-9449
Fax: 208-336-5559

Illinois

Chicagoland Apartment Association
4825 N. Scott, Suite 119
Schiller Park, IL 60176
Phone: 847-678-5717
Fax: 847-678-5731
Web site: <www.caapts.org>

Illinois Apartment Association
4825 N. Scott, Suite 119
Schiller Park, IL 60176
Phone: 847-678-5717
Fax: 847-678-5731

Indiana

Apartment Association of East Central
    Indiana
P.O. Box 1129
Muncie, IN 47308-1129
Phone: 765-288-2492
Fax: 765-286-7349
Web site: <www.rentmuncie.com>

Apartment Association of Fort Wayne/
    NE Indiana
6155 Stoney Creek Dr.
Fort Wayne, IN 46825
Phone: 260-482-2916
Fax: 260-482-5187
Web site: <www.apartmentsfort
    wayne.com>

Apartment Association of Indiana
9202 N. Meridian, Suite 250
Indianapolis, IN 46260
Phone: 317-816-8900
Fax: 317-816-8911
Web site: <www.aptassociation
indiana.org>

Apartment Association of Southern
Indiana, Inc.
P.O. Box 5526
Evansville, IN 47716-5526
Phone: 812-473-0917
Fax: 812-473-6401
Web site: <www.aaosi.com>

Apartment Association of Terre Haute
839 East Jackson St.
Sullivan, IN 47882
Phone: 812-268-5518

Clinton County Property Managers
859 Walsh Ave.
Frankfort, IN 46041
Phone: 765-659-5485
Fax: 765-659-5878

Howard County Apartment Association
3334 Dixon Lane
Kokomo, IN 46902
Phone: 317-455-0250
Fax: 317-453-5990

Monroe County Apartment Association
P.O. Box 202
Bloomington, IN 47402
Phone: 812-332-7363
Fax: 812-339-0138
Web site: <www.mcaaonline.org>

Northern Indiana Apartment Council
9202 N. Meridian, Suite 200
Indianapolis, IN 46260
Phone: 317-571-5600
Fax: 317-571-5603

Riverbend Apartment Association
19886 Miller Rd.
South Bend, IN 46614
Phone: 219-289-7785

Tippecanoe Apartment Association
983 South Creasy Lane
Lafayette, IN 47905
Phone: 765-464-3800

Iowa

National Apartment Association
201 North Union St., Suite 200
Alexandria, VA 22314
Phone: 703-518-6141

Kansas

Apartment Association of Greater
Wichita
949 S. Glendale, #400
Wichita, KS 67218
Phone: 316-682-3508
Fax: 316-684-4080

Apartment Association of Kansas City
11338 Shawnee Mission Pkwy
Shawnee Mission, MO 66203
Phone: 913-248-0355
Fax: 913-248-0882

Apartment Association of Topeka
P.O. Box 3845
Topeka, KS 66604
Phone: 785-273-1392
Fax: 785-273-3319
Web site: <www.ACTopeka.org>

Kansas (State) Apartment Association
949 S Glendale-Parklane, #400
Wichita, KS 67218
Phone: 316-682-3508
Fax: 316-684-4080

Kentucky

Greater Lexington Apartment
  Association
210 Malabu Dr., #7
Lexington, KY 40502
Phone: 859-278-6540
Fax: 859-277-9187
Web site: <www.lexaptassoc.com>

Greater Cincinnati & Northern
  Kentucky Apartment Association
525 W. 5th St., Suite 233
Covington, KY 41011
Phone: 859-581-5990
Fax: 859-581-5993
Web site: <www.gcnkaa.org>

Louisville Apartment Association
7400 S. Park Pl., #1
Louisville, KY 40222
Phone: 502-426-6140
Fax: 502-426-2148
Web site: <www.laaky.com>

Louisiana

Acadiana Apartment Association
P.O. Box 53741
Lafayette, LA 70505
Phone: 337-235-6080
Fax: 337-235-6029

Apartment Association of Greater New
  Orleans
3017 Harvard Ave., #201
Metairie, LA 70006
Phone: 504-888-2492
Fax: 504-888-2601
Web site: <www.aagno.com>

Apartment Association of Louisiana
515 South College Rd., #210
Lafayette, LA 70503
Phone: 337-237-3773
Fax: 337-235-6029

Baton Rouge Apartment Association
1933 Wooddale Blvd., #K-1
Baton Rouge, LA 70806-1514
Phone: 225-923-2808
Fax: 225-927-8159
Web site: <www.braa.com>

Houma-Thibodau Apartment
  Association
425 W. Tunnel Blvd.
Houma, LA 70360
Phone: 985-879-2772
Fax: 985-879-2726
Web site: <www.houmathibodaux
  apts.com>

Northeast Louisiana Apartment
  Association
P.O. Box 8461
Monroe, LA 71211
Phone: 318-322-9927
Fax: 318-322-9931

Shreveport-Bossier Apartment
  Association
P.O. Box 5938
Shreveport, LA 71135-5938
Phone: 318-677-4229
Fax: 318-868-5845

Southwest Louisiana Apartment
  Association
P.O. Box 6534
Lake Charles, LA 70606
Phone: 337-477-2851
Fax: 337-478-1148

Maine

National Apartment Association
201 North Union St., Suite 200
Alexandria, VA 22314
Phone: 703-518-6141

Maryland

Apartment & Office Building
    Association (AOBA)
1050 17th St., NW, #300
Washington, DC 20036
Phone: 202-296-3390
Fax: 202-296-3399

Massachusetts

Greater Boston Real Estate Board
11 Beacon St., 1st Floor
Boston, MA 02108
Phone: 617-668-8282
Fax: 617-338-2600
Web site: <www.gbreb.com>

Michigan

Detroit Metropolitan Apartment
    Association
26899 Northwestern Hwy, Suite 120
Southfield, MI 48034-8419
Phone: 248-799-9151
Fax: 248-799-5497

Property Management Association of
    Michigan
2757 44th St., #104
Wyoming, MI 49509-4192
Phone: 616-970-0399
Fax: 616-257-0398
Web site: <www.pmamhq.com>

Property Management Association of
    Eastern Michigan
P.O. Box 884
Grand Blanc, MI 48439
Phone: 810-513-5073

Property Management Association of
    Mid-Michigan
P.O. Box 27011
Lansing, MI 48909-7011
Phone: 517-485-1917
Fax: 517-647-7451
Web site: <www.pmamm.com>

Property Management Association of
    West Michigan
2757 44th St., #306
Wyoming, MI 49509
Phone: 616-531-5243
Fax: 616-257-0398
Web site: <www.pmawm.com>

Washtenaw Area Apartment Association
179 Little Lake Dr.
Ann Arbor, MI 48103
Phone: 743-663-1200
Fax: 743-996-1008
Web site: <www.mlive.com/
    apartments/aaaaa/>

Minnesota

National Apartment Association
201 North Union St., Suite 200
Alexandria, VA 22314
Phone: 703-518-6141

Mississippi

National Apartment Association
201 North Union St., Suite 200
Alexandria, VA 22314
Phone: 703-518-6141

Missouri

Apartment Association of Kansas City
11338 Shawnee Mission Pkwy
Shawnee Mission, MO 66203
Phone: 913-248-0355
Fax: 913-248-0882

Columbia Apartment Association
P.O. Box 1504
Columbia, MO 65205
Phone: 573-815-1150
Fax: 573-815-7573

Mid Missouri Rental Properties
  Association
P.O. Box 977
Rolla, MO 64501
Phone: 573-364-1985
Fax: 573-364-5836

Mid-Missouri Apartment Association
820 Southwest Blvd.
Jefferson City, MO 65109
Phone: 573-636-3168
Fax: 573-636-3705

Missouri Apartment Association
P.O. Box 480187
Kansas City, MO 64148
Phone: 888-859-5192
Fax: 816-941-3296
Web site: <www.moapts.org>

Saint Louis Apartment Association
12777 Olive Blvd., #B
St. Louis, MO 63141
Phone: 314-205-8844
Fax: 314-205-1410
Web site: <www.slaa.org>

Southwest Missouri Rental Housing
  Association
P.O. Box 1801
Joplin, MO 64802
Phone: 417-437-3839
Fax: 417-782-5212
Web site: <www.swmorent.com>

Springfield Apartment & Housing
  Association
P.O. Box 10945
Springfield, MO 65808
Phone: 417-883-4942
Fax: 417-886-3685
Web site: <www.springfield
  housing.net>

Montana

National Apartment Association
201 North Union St., Suite 200
Alexandria, VA 22314
Phone: 703-518-6141

Nebraska

Apartment Association of Greater
  Omaha
P.O. Box 540705
Omaha, NE 68154
Phone: 402-968-8360
Fax: 402-965-3372
Web site: <www.aagomaha.org>

Nevada

Northern Nevada Apartment Association
1 East First St., Suite 1105
Reno, NV 89501
Phone: 775-322-6622
Fax: 775-322-9860
Web site: <www.nnaa.info>

New Hampshire

New Hampshire Multi-Family Housing
  Association
P.O. Box 321
Manchester, NH 03105
Phone: 603-668-8282
Fax: 603-647-6133

New Jersey

New Jersey Apartment Association
197 Route 18 South, #230
East Brunswick, NJ 08816
Phone: 732-247-6661
Fax: 732-247-6669
Web site: <www.njaa.com>

New Mexico

Apartment Association of New Mexico
6755 Academy Rd., NE, Suite B
Albuquerque, NM 87109-3345
Phone: 505-822-1114
Fax: 505-822-8557
Web site: <www.aanm.com>

New York

Apartment Council of Western New York
142 Bauman Rd.
Williamsville, NY 14221
Phone: 716-633-0959
Fax: 716-631-0899
Web site: <www.acwny.com>

North Carolina

Apartment Association of North Carolina
2101 Rexford Rd., #330-E
Charlotte, NC 28211
Phone: 704-334-9511
Fax: 704-333-4221

Charlotte Apartment Association
2101 Rexford Rd., #330-E
Charlotte, NC 28211
Phone: 704-344-9511
Fax: 704-333-4221
Web site: <www.charlotteapartment
   assn.org>

Cumberland County Apartment
   Association
P.O. Box 9417
Fayetteville, NC 28311
Phone: 910-829-1843
Fax: 910-822-0510

Greater Asheville Area Apartment
   Association
P.O. Box 846
Asheville, NC 28802
Phone: 828-277-7290
Fax: 828-277-7293

Greenville Area Property Managers
P.O. Box 275
Greenville, NC 27835-0275
Phone: 252-758-1921
Fax: 252-355-4973

Triad Apartment Association
3407 - E West Wendover Ave.
Greensboro, NC 27407
Phone: 336-294-4428
Fax: 336-294-4481
Web site: <www.taa.bz>

Triangle Apartment Association
3739 National Dr., #202
Raleigh, NC 27612
Phone: 919-782-1165
Fax: 919-782-1169
Web site: <www.triangleaptassn.org>

Wilmington Apartment Association
P.O. Box 3413
Wilmington, NC 28403
Phone: 910-799-8580
Fax: 910-452-2650

North Dakota

Bismarck-Mandan Apartment Association
P.O. Box 1793
Bismarck, ND 58502-1793
Phone: 701-255-7396
Fax: 701-222-0103
Web site: <www.bisman-apts.com>

FM Apartment Association
P.O. Box 11342
Fargo, ND 58107-2025
Phone: 218-233-6245
Fax: 218-233-6245

North Dakota Apartment Association
P.O. Box 2317
Bismarck, ND 58502
Phone: 701-221-2751
Fax: 701-224-9824

Ohio

Columbus Apartment Association
1225 Dublin Rd.
Columbus, OH 43215
Phone: 614-488-2115
Fax: 614-488-8526
Web site: <www.columbusapts.org>

Greater Dayton Apartment Association
2555 South Dixie Dr., #100
Dayton, OH 45409-1532
Phone: 937-293-1170
Fax: 937-293-1180
Web site: <www.gdaa.org>

Greater Cincinnati & Northern
  Kentucky Apartment Association
525 W 5th St., Suite 233
Covington, KY 41011
Phone: 859-581-5990
Fax: 859-581-5993
Web site: <www.gcnkaa.org>

Ohio Apartment Association
1225 Dublin Rd.
Columbus, OH 43215
Phone: 614-294-4222
Fax: 614-421-6887

Oklahoma

Apartment Association of Central
  Oklahoma
3750 West Main St., #112
Norman, OK 73072
Phone: 405-701-1710
Fax: 405-701-1719

Oklahoma Multi Housing Association
718 NW 17th St.
Oklahoma City, OK 73103
Phone: 405-840-9855
Fax: 405-840-9838

Stillwater Apartment Association
P.O. Box 882
Stillwater, OK 74076
Phone: 405-372-8862
Fax: 405-372-8862

Tulsa Apartment Association
6855 South Canton
Tulsa, OK 74136-3405
Phone: 918-747-6217
Fax: 918-747-6244
Web site: <www.taaonline.org>

Oregon

National Apartment Association
201 North Union St., Suite 200
Alexandria, VA 22314
Phone: 703-518-6141

Pennsylvania

Apartment Association of Central
  Pennsylvania
644 Allenview Dr.
Mechanicsburg, PA 17055-6181
Phone: 717-691-8984
Fax: 717-691-8984

Apartment Association of Greater
  Philadelphia
One Bala Plaza, Suite 515
Bala Cynwyd, PA 19004
Phone: 610-664-1800
Fax: 610-664-4481
Web site: <www.aapg.com>

Rhode Island

National Apartment Association
201 North Union St., Suite 200
Alexandria, VA 22314
Phone: 703-518-6141

South Carolina

Apartment Association of Greater
  Columbia
P.O. Box 7515
Columbia, SC 29202
Phone: 803-252-5032
Fax: 803-252-0589

Charleston Apartment Association
P.O. Box 1763
Columbia, SC 29202
Phone: 843-722-7585
Fax: 803-252-0589

Myrtle Beach Apartment Association
P.O. Box 2752
Myrtle Beach, SC 29588
Phone: 843-293-7256
Fax: 843-293-9001

South Carolina Apartment Association
P.O. Box 7515
Columbia, SC 29202
Phone: 803-252-5032
Fax: 803-252-0589

Upper State Apartment Association
535 N. Pleasantburg Dr., #202
Greenville, SC 29607
Phone: 864-242-0200
Fax: 864-233-2807

South Dakota

Black Hills Area Multi-Housing
  Association
P.O. Box 434
Rapid City, SD 57709
Phone: 605-336-7756
Fax: 605-330-0500

South Dakota Multi-Housing Association
812 S. Minnesota Ave.
Sioux Falls, SD 57104
Phone: 605-336-7756
Fax: 605-336-7756

Tennessee

Apartment Association of Greater
  Knoxville
5410 Homberg Dr., #17-A
Knoxville, TN 37919
Phone: 865-588-8961
Fax: 865-588-7905
Web site: <www.akag.org>

Chattanooga Apartment Association
P.O. Box 4367
Chattanooga, TN 37405
Phone: 423-876-8121
Fax: 423-877-9846

Greater Nashville Apartment Association
810 Royal Pkwy Dr., Suite 110
Nashville, TN 37214
Phone: 615-883-9941
Fax: 615-883-1922

Tennessee Apartment Association
810 Royal Pkwy Dr., Suite 110
Nashville, TN 37214
Phone: 615-883-9941
Fax: 615-883-1922

Tri-City Apartment Association
P.O. Box 981
Johnson City, TN 37605
Phone: 423-926-4156
Fax: 423-926-5530

Texas

Apartment Association of Tarrant
  County, Inc.
6350 Baker Blvd.
Fort Worth, TX 76118
Phone: 817-284-1121
Fax: 817-284-2054

Apartment Association of the Permian
  Basin
P.O. Box 12392
Odessa, TX 79768
Phone: 915-333-7133
Fax: 915-332-2209

Apartment Association of Central Texas
1920 N. Main, #102
Belton, TX 76513
Phone: 254-939-5655
Fax: 254-939-6664

Apartment Association of Greater Dallas
4230 LBJ Freeway, #140
Dallas, TX 75244-5804
Phone: 972-385-9091
Fax: 972-385-9412
Web site: <www.aagdallas.com>

Apartment Association of SE Texas
985 IH-10 North
Beaumont, TX 77706
Phone: 409-899-4455
Fax: 409-899-1507
Web site: <www.setxaa.org>

Apartment Association of the Panhandle
5601 Enterprise Circle, Suite D
Amarillo, TX 79106-4631
Phone: 806-355-6391
Fax: 806-355-0451

Austin Apartment Association
4107 Medical Pkwy, #100
Austin, TX 78756
Phone: 512-323-0990
Fax: 512-323-2979
Web site: <www.austinaptassoc.com>

Big County Apartment Association
P.O. Box 7045
Abilene, TX 79608
Phone: 915-695-7431
Fax: 915-659-3489
Web site: <www.bigcountry
  apartments.com>

Bryan-College Station Apartment
  Association
1808 Barak Lane
Bryan, TX 77802-3448
Phone: 979-260-9842
Fax: 979-260-2894
Web site: <www.bcsaa.com>

Corpus Christi Apartment Association
4630 Corona Dr., #35
Corpus Christi, TX 78411-4315
Phone: 361-852-4226
Fax: 361-852-0763
Web site: <www.ccapts.org>

Corsicana Apartment Association
1025 North 24th St.
Corsicana, TX 75110
Phone: 903-874-7165
Fax: 903-872-8267
Web site: <www.Corsicana
  Apartments.org>

El Paso Apartment Association
1155 Larry Mahan, #H-2
El Paso, TX 79925
Phone: 915-598-0800
Fax: 915-598-1881
Web site: <www.epaa.org>

Galveston County Apartment
  Association
P.O. Box 3934
Galveston, TX 77552
Phone: 409-762-8339
Fax: 409-762-6345

Greater Longview Apartment
  Association
2127 Gilmer Rd.
Longview, TX 75604
Phone: 903-759-3966
Fax: 903-759-5516

Heart of Texas Apartment Association
P.O. Box 8250
Waco, TX 76714
Phone: 254-776-5451
Fax: 254-776-5877

Houston Apartment Association
10815 Fallstone Rd.
Houston, TX 77099-3496
Phone: 281-933-2224
Fax: 281-933-8412
Web site: <www.haaonline.org>

Lubbock Apartment Association
4227-85th St.
Lubbock, TX 79423
Phone: 806-794-2037
Fax: 806-794-9597
Web site: <www.lubbock
  apartments.com>

Midland Apartment Association
P.O. Box 9534
Midland, TX 79708
Phone: 915-699-5265
Fax: 915-694-0707
Web site: <www.rentmidland.com>

North Texas Rental Properties
  Association
2403 9th St.
Wichita Falls, TX 76301
Phone: 940-322-7667
Fax: 940-723-0896

Piney Woods Apartment Association
P.O. Box 631280
Nacogdoches, TX 75963-1280
Phone: 936-560-2211
Fax: 936-569-1883

Rio Grande Valley Apartment
  Association
902 E. Tyler, Suite C
Harlingen, TX 78551-3299
Phone: 956-428-5072
Fax: 956-412-6192
Web site: <www.rgvaa.org>

San Angelo Apartment Association, Inc.
P.O. Box 3282
San Angelo, TX 76902
Phone: 915-942-1332
Fax: 915-942-6529

San Antonio Apartment Association
4204 Gardendale, #200
San Antonio, TX 78229
Phone: 210-692-7797
Fax: 210-692-7277
Web site: <www.saaaonline.org>

Texarkana Apartment Association
P.O. Box 1378
Texarkana, TX 75504-1378
Phone: 903-793-7533
Fax: 903-791-0923

Texas Apartment Association
606 W 12th St.
Austin, TX 78701
Phone: 512-479-6252
Fax: 512-479-6291

Tyler Apartment Association
1600 Rice Rd.
Tyler, TX 75703
Phone: 903-581-0082
Fax: 903-561-3463
Web site: <www.taa.org>

Victoria Apartment Association
P.O. Box 7192
Victoria, TX 77902
Phone: 361-578-2954
Fax: 361-578-0671

Utah

National Apartment Association
201 North Union St., Suite 200
Alexandria, VA 22314
Phone: 703-518-6141

Vermont

National Apartment Association
201 North Union St., Suite 200
Alexandria, VA 22314
Phone: 703-518-6141

Virginia

Apartment & Office Building
  Association (AOBA)
1050 17th St., NW, #300
Washington, DC 20036
Phone: 202-296-3390
Fax: 202-296-3399
Web site: <www.aoba-metro.org>

Blue Ridge Apartment Council
PMB 230, 977 Seminole Trail
Charlottesville, VA 22901-2824
Phone: 804-977-3033
Fax: 804-979-4826
Web site: <www.brac.com>

Fredericksburg Area Multihousing
  Association
P.O. Box 1495
Midlothian, VA 23113
Phone: 804-273-0845
Fax: 804-747-8465

Valley Landlords Association
640 Maple Ave.
Waynesboro, VA 22980
Phone: 540-943-3555
Fax: 540-943-3555

New River Valley Apartment Council
301 Hunt Club Rd., #6800
Blacksburg, VA 24060
Phone: 540-951-1221
Fax: 540-951-9302

Roanoke Valley Apartment Association
1650 Lancing Dr., #55
Roanoke, VA 24153
Phone: 540-389-0209
Fax: 540-389-4495
Web site: <www.apt-guide.com/rvaa>

Virginia Apartment & Management
  Association
8611 Mayland Dr.
Richmond, VA 23294
Phone: 804-288-2899
Fax: 804-288-4022
Web site: <www.vamaonline.org>

Washington

National Apartment Association
201 North Union St., Suite 200
Alexandria, VA 22314
Phone: 703-518-6141

West Virginia

National Apartment Association
201 North Union St., Suite 200
Alexandria, VA 22314
Phone: 703-518-6141

Wisconsin

Apartment Owners & Managers
  Association of Milwaukee
701 N. Plankinton Ave., Suite 207
Milwaukee, WI 53203
Phone: 414-278-7557
Fax: 414-271-6126

Wausau Area Apartment Association
P.O. Box 723
Wausau, WI 54402-0723
Phone: 715-359-1500
Fax: 715-355-0028
Web site: <www.apartmentassociation
  online.com>

Wyoming

National Apartment Association
201 North Union St., Suite 200
Alexandria, VA 22314
Phone: 703-518-6141

GLOSSARY

ACCOMMODATOR A neutral third party that assists in completing a delayed 1031 tax-deferred exchange. The accommodator is usually a corporate entity.

ACTIVE INVESTOR An IRS classification for a real estate investor who materially participates in running a property.

ADJUSTABLE-RATE MORTGAGE (ARM) A loan in which the future interest rate may change, with that change determined by an index of rates. The frequency and amount of change are limited by the mortgage contract.

ADJUSTED COST BASIS For the purpose of computing capital gains or losses, the adjusted cost basis is the original purchase price plus closing costs paid at the time of purchase, plus the cost value of improvements done while the property was held, less all depreciation claimed.

ADJUSTED GROSS INCOME The income from a piece of property after any adjustments are made for other income or rental losses.

ADJUSTED SALES PRICE The price of a property after deducting the costs of sale.

APPRAISAL The process of estimating the current market value of a property.

APPRECIATION Increase in value due to any cause.

AMORTIZATION   The repayment terms of a loan, including the required principal and interest, based on the interest rate and the period of time allowed to pay down, or amortize, the loan to zero.

ANNUAL DEPRECIATION ALLOWANCE   The deduction you can take on your income tax against earnings to recapture the cost of the structures on your property.

ANNUAL EXPENSES   All the costs that you must pay to operate your property.

AVERAGE RETURN ON EQUITY (AROE)   Each year that you own a property you can calculate the return on the equity for that year. Add up the returns for several years and divide by the number of years to get the average.

BASIS   The cost of the building on your property, plus improvements and fixtures, which can be depreciated but not claimed as deductions. Basis is calculated as original cost plus capital improvements less depreciation.

BOOT   An IRS term for taxable proceeds from a sale other than cash.

CAP   A limit on the amount of increase a lender may impose under the terms of an adjustable-rate mortgage. The annual cap specifies the maximum annual increase, and the lifetime cap specifies the overall increase the lender is allowed to pass on to the borrower.

CAPITAL EXPENSE   The outlay to purchase any asset with a useful life of over one year (the tax treatment for such expenditure allows the asset to be "capitalized," which means the cost is deducted over its useful life, according to the applicable depreciation method rather than as an expense in the current period.

CAPITAL GAINS   The profit you make on an investment.

CAPITALIZATION OF INCOME   A valuation method achieved by dividing the net income of a property by the capitalization rate of that kind of property.

CAPITALIZATION RATE   The percentage return that you get by dividing the net income from a property by the price of the property.

CASH FLOW   The amount of money received from rental income each month less the amount paid out in mortgage payments, the purchase of capital assets, and payment of any operating expenses. Cash flow is not the same as profit, because it includes nondeductible payments.

CASH-ON-CASH RETURN   The cash profit from an investment divided by the cash invested to buy the investment.

COLLECTED RENT   Amount of rental income actually collected.

COMMERCIAL LOANS   Any loan not classified as a residential loan, usually on five units or more.

COMMERCIAL PROPERTY   Nonresidential property operated for business use.

COMPARABLES (COMPS)   Properties that are similar to the property being considered or appraised.

COMPARATIVE ANALYSIS   A method of appraisal in which selling prices of similar properties are used as the basis for arriving at the value estimate. It is also known as the market data approach.

COMPOUND INTEREST   Interest paid on original principal and also on the accrued interest.

COMPOUND INTEREST ALGORITHM   A mathematical formula used to calculate the percentage return when profits from an investment are reinvested over a given period of time.

COST BASIS   Your basis for calculating the capital gain on a property you own.

DEBT COVERAGE   The comparison between the net income of a property and the loan payments on the property.

DELAYED EXCHANGE   An IRS-approved technique for completing an exchange of equity to postpone taxes. Also called a "Starker" exchange.

DEMAND APPRECIATION   Appreciation in value related to an increase in the desire to possess the property.

DEPARTMENT OF VETERANS AFFAIRS   The federal government agency that administers GI or VA loans. Previously known as the Veterans Administration or VA.

DEPRECIABLE IMPROVEMENTS   The value of the structures on a property that the IRS allows you to depreciate.

DEPRECIATED VALUE   The value that remains after deducting the depreciation from the cost base for a property.

DEPRECIATION   Loss of value due to any cause, as an appraisal term.

DEPRECIATION ALLOWANCE   The dollar amount the IRS allows you to deduct each year from the earnings from a property.

EQUITY   The portion of real estate you own. In the case of a property bought for $200,000 with a $133,000 mortgage owing, the equity is the difference, or $67,000.

EQUITY GROWTH FROM APPRECIATION   The increase in a property's value because of the effects of inflation.

EQUITY GROWTH FROM LOAN REDUCTION   The increase in the owner's equity in a property from the payoff of the financing.

FEDERAL HOUSING ADMINISTRATION (FHA)   An agency created by the National Housing Act of 1934 to provide a home-financing system through federal mortgage insurance.

FIXED EXPENSES   The regular recurring costs required in holding a property, such as taxes and insurance.

FIXED-RATE LOAN   A loan in which the interest rate will not change during the contract period as a matter of contract.

FULLY AMORTIZED   Refers to a loan that is completely paid off when all the payments are made.

GI LOAN   A guaranteed loan available to veterans under a federal government program administered by the Department of Veterans Affairs. Also called a VA loan.

GROSS RENT MULTIPLIER   A factor used for appraising income-producing property. The multiplier times the gross income gives an approximate property value.

HIGHEST AND BEST USE   The use of property for the most profitable, efficient, and appropriate purpose, given the zoning and other restrictions placed on the land.

IMPROVEMENTS   Any structure or addition to a piece of raw land.

INFLATION   An economic condition occurring when the money supply increases in relation to goods and associated with rising wages and costs and decreasing purchasing power.

INFLATIONARY APPRECIATION   Refers to the value of a product increasing due to inflation taking place in the economy.

INSTALLMENT NOTE   The name of the note carried by a seller of a property that gives the seller special tax benefits

INSTALLMENT SALE   The sale of a property where the seller carries an installment note.

INVEST   To commit money or capital in business in order to earn a financial return; the outlay of money for income or profit.

LAND SALES CONTRACT   Another name for conditional sales contract. The buyer takes possession, and the seller retains title until all conditions are met.

LEVERAGE   The use of borrowed money to purchase an investment that realizes enough income to cover the expense of the financing, with the excess accruing to the purchaser.

MARGIN   The number that is added to the index of a loan to get the final interest rate of the loan.

MODIFIED ACCELERATED COST RECOVERY SYSTEM (MACRS)   The IRS system for determining the depreciation schedule for capital items.

MORTGAGE   A contract that makes a specific property the security for payment of a debt.

"NEG-AM" LOANS   Loans where you have the option to pay a lower payment than is needed to pay all the interest due.

NEGATIVE AMORTIZATION   Occurs when the payments on an adjustable loan are not sufficient to pay all the interest due. In this case, the loan increases by the amount of the unpaid interest.

"NO-NEG" LOANS   Loans where the payment will always pay all the interest due on the loan.

OPERATING EXPENSES   Periodic expenditures necessary to maintain the property and continue the production of effective gross income.

PASSIVE INVESTORS   An IRS term that refers to someone who is limited in the deductions that can be claimed against earnings.

POINT   One percent of the loan amount; an additional charge added on by a lender as a fee assessed for getting the loan. Points are also called "loan fees."

POSITIVE CASH FLOW   A situation in which cash receipts are greater than cash payments.

RENT SURVEY   A survey done to find out what other owners are charging for rent in a given area.

RESPA   The Real Estate Settlement Procedures Act, a federal law that ensures that buyers and sellers in certain federally related residential real estate transactions receive full disclosure of all settlement costs, so they can shop around for settlement services.

RETURN ON EQUITY (ROE)   A percentage of return calculated by dividing annual net income by equity.

RETURN ON INVESTMENT (ROI)   Interest or profit from an investment.

SCHEDULED RENT   The current rent scheduled for all the units in a building.

SECTION 8   The federal government's principal medium for housing assistance, authorized by the Housing and Community Development Act of 1974, which provides for new construction and rehabilitation.

STARKER EXCHANGE   A type of tax-deferred exchange that got its name from the court case of the same name. Also called a "delayed" exchange.

STRAIGHT NOTE   A note in which the amount of the loan and the interest are paid with only one payment.

TAX BENEFITS   The tax savings from property ownership.

TAX-DEFERRED EXCHANGE (1031 TAX-DEFERRED EXCHANGE)   A method of deferring capital gains by exchanging real property for other like-kind property.

TAX SHELTER   An investment with paper losses that can be used to lower one's otherwise taxable income. In other words, the tax loss from the tax-shelter investment is a write-off against regular salary or other income and therefore "shelters" that income.

THREE-PARTY EXCHANGE   A tax-deferred exchange that involves three different parties.

TURNOVER   When one tenant moves out of a property and another moves in; usually means no loss of rent.

UP-LEG PROPERTY   The larger property in a tax-deferred exchange.

U.S. DEPARTMENT OF HOUSING AND URBAN DEVELOPMENT (HUD)   A government agency established in 1965 that provides federal assistance in planning, developing, and managing public housing.

USEFUL LIFE   For tax purposes, this is the period of time over which you must depreciate a property. As a general concept, this is the period of time a property is expected to be functional.

VACANCY RATE   The average percentage of units that are vacant in a given market area.

VALUE APPRECIATION   The increase in value of a property from all causes.

VARIABLE EXPENSES   Expenses on a property, which tend to be different each month or pay period.

VETERANS ADMINISTRATION (VA)   A government agency that is set up to help individuals who have served in the armed forces; now part of the Department of Veterans Affairs.

RECOMMENDED READING

Allen, Robert G. *Multiple Streams of Income.* Hoboken, N.J.: John Wiley & Sons, 2000.

Bronchick, William, and Robert Dahlstrom. *Flipping Properties: Generate Instant Cash Profits in Real Estate.* Chicago: Dearborn Trade Publishing, 2001.

Conti, Peter, and David Finkel. *Making Big Money Investing in Real Estate.* Chicago: Dearborn Trade Publishing, 2002.

Edwards, Brian F., and Casey Edwards. *The Complete Idiot's Guide to Being a Smart Landlord.* New York: Alpha Books, 2000.

Griswold, Robert S. *Property Management for Dummies.* Hoboken, N.J.: John Wiley & Sons, 2001.

Kiyosaki, Robert, and Dolf de Roos. *Real Estate Riches: How to Become Rich Using Your Banker's Money.* New York: Warner Books, 2001.

Kiyosaki, Robert, and Sharon Lechter. *Rich Dad, Poor Dad: What the Rich Teach Their Kids About Money That the Poor and Middle Class Do Not!* New York: Warner Books, 2000.

Kiyosaki, Robert, and Sharon L. Lechter. *Cash Flow Quadrant: Rich Dad's Guide to Financial Freedom.* New York: Warner Books, 2000.

McClean, Andrew, and Gary W. Eldrid. *Investing in Real Estate.* 3d ed. Hoboken, N.J.: John Wiley & Sons, 2001.

Patton, David, and Leigh Robinson. *Landlording: A Handymanual for Scrupulous Landlords and Landladies Who Do It Themselves.* 9th ed. Newbury, U.K.: Express Publishing, 2001.

Perry, Greg M. *Managing Rental Properties for Maximum Profit.* Roseville, Calif.: Prima Publishing, 2000.

Strauss, Spencer, and Martin Stone. *The Unofficial Guide to Real Estate Investing.* Hoboken, N.J.: John Wiley & Sons, 1999.

Strauss, Steven D. *Ask a Lawyer: Landlord and Tenant.* New York: W.W. Norton & Co., 1998.

Vollucci, Eugene E. *How to Buy and Sell Apartment Buildings.* Hoboken, N.J.: John Wiley & Sons, 1993.

INDEX

ABOUT THE AUTHORS

Martin Stone is the coauthor of *The Unofficial Guide to Real Estate Investing* (John Wiley & Sons, 1999). A graduate of USC with a degree in finance, Marty has built more than 40 multifamily apartment buildings, managed more that 1,000 units, and written and lectured extensively about all areas related to real estate investing over the past 30 years. He is also the managing broker of Buckingham Real Estate Investments and Richmond Financial Services in El Segundo, California. Marty lives with his wife, Lori, in a home he built himself. Feel free to contact him by e-mail at gr8profit@aol.com, or visit the office Web site at <www.buckinghaminvestments.com>.

Spencer Strauss makes his living as a real estate broker working side-by-side with his writing partner, Martin Stone. In that capacity, Spencer has bought, sold, traded, and managed countless buildings and has helped scores of investors get their start in real estate. Besides coauthoring *The Unofficial Guide to Real Estate Investing,* Spencer also cowrote *The Complete Idiot's Guide to Impeachment of the President* (Macmillan Publishing, 1998). He has been featured on television on *KABC Eyewitness News,* as well as on radio stations KFI and KABC, all in Southern California. Additionally, Spencer's analysis has been featured in *USA Today,* the *New York Post,* the *Chicago Tribune,* the *Long Beach Press Telegram,* and the *Los Angeles Times.* Spencer can be contacted for free real estate advice via e-mail at spence@spencerstrauss.com.